Fifty Years AFTER

John Gardam
OMM, CD, BA

Forewords: General J.A. Dextraze, CC, CBE, CMM, DSO, CD
General P.D. Manson, CMM, CD
Vice Admiral J.A. Fulton, CMM, CD

GSPH

Fifty Years After

Published by

GENERAL STORE
PUBLISHING HOUSE INC.

1 Main Street, Burnstown, Ontario, Canada K0J 1G0
Telephone (613)432-7697   Fax (613)432-7184

ISBN 0-919431-41-0
Printed and bound in Canada.

Cover Design and Layout by Hugh Malcolm

Copyright ©1990
The General Store Publishing House Inc.
Burnstown, Ontario, Canada

General Store Publishing House Inc. gratefully acknowledges the assistance of the Ontario Arts Council.

Canadian Cataloguing in Publication Data

Gardam, John, 1931-
Fifty years after

ISBN 0-919431-41-0

1. World War, 1939-1945--Personal narratives, Canadian. 2. World War, 1939-1945--Canada.

D811.A2G37 1990   940.53'71   C90-090400-3

First Printing August 1990

*I dedicate this book to all those veterans
who gave me their wartime stories.
May their contribution to Canada never be forgotten.*

Fifty Years After

All profits received by the author from the sale of this book will be donated to the Canadian Forces Personnel Assistance Fund to aid sailors, soldiers, air personnel, and other men and women of the Canadian Forces who are in financial distress.

Some front cover drawings adapted from Tools of War, Reader's Digest Association (Canada) Ltd.

Back cover photograph: Author receiving 3rd clasp (42 years service) to Canadian Forces Decoration, 28 February 1990, from Chief of the Defence Staff, General John de Chastelaine, CMM, CD (Armed Forces photograph)

By the same author:

The National War Memorial
(Veterans Affairs Canada. 1982)

Seventy Years After 1914 - 1984.
(Canada's Wings Inc., 1983)

The Legacy
(Department of National Defence, 1988)

Contents

Forewords

General J.A. Dextraze, CC, CBE, CMM, DSO, CD
Former Chief of the Defence Staff

When I read the manuscript of this book in May 1990, I found it difficult to concentrate on the matter at hand, writing this foreword. Here was a book about Canadians at war, their triumphs and sacrifices, but foremost in my mind was a phone call from my seven-year-old grandson. He wanted to know why the rest of Canada celebrated Victoria Day, when to him it was a day off school while his teachers had a professional development day. It struck me that history had not brought unified results for all our Canadian celebrations.

Deep in my heart, I trust that those who read this book, regardless of their linguistic background, will remember the well over one million Canadian brothers and sisters who wore uniform in the Second World War. Over 42,000 Canadians gave their lives to preserve our freedom and to protect the colourful history of Canada. Canadians must not misuse this freedom so dearly paid for.

When I was in Normandy, France, recently, I went back to Falaise, where I had fought as Company Commander with Les Fusiliers Mont-Royal. After walking the battlefields of so long ago, I visited the Canadian cemetery at Bretteville-sur-Laize. There, I came upon the grave and headstone of Private Gerard Doré of Roberval, Quebec. He was but sixteen when he died by my side some forty-six years ago on 23 July 1944. I wondered how I could have explained to him the political situation in Canada. I would have been ashamed to tell him of today's balance-sheet of achievements. Though a boy in years, Gerard acted as a man in freely giving his life for his country; today's political leaders, bent on rationalizing only their own regional views

Fifty Years After

General J.A. Dextrze, Chief of Defence Staff, converses with LCol J. Gardam, Commandant Canadian Forces Officer Candidate School, Chilliwack, B.C. 1974
CF Photo

rather than considering their country, seem immature in comparison.

Fifty Years After is a "must read" book. Author John Gardam deserves the respect of all Canadians.

General P.D. Manson, CMM, CD
Former Chief of the Defence Staff

As historians well know, time has a way of bringing clarity to great events. World War Two was wrapped in complexity, secrecy and human emotion when it happened. Countless books were written at the time and in the decades to follow, but it was only gradually that a thorough understanding emerged. Today, fifty years later, one can read many learned and lucid accounts of the causes, conduct and consequences of that great conflict.

In one respect, however, time has a regrettable effect on such writings. Quite naturally, as masses of data are distilled into the really key elements of history, the story becomes largely one of great battles, strategies, weapons, statesmen and generals. The human dimension of war, particularly as it relates to "ordinary" people, tends to give way to other more prominent aspects. This is understandable, to be sure. Memories fade, and the human mind has a blessed attribute of suppressing horror of the kind that was so abundant in the Second World War. Besides, old soldiers do die, and many have taken their untold stories with them to the grave.

Thankfully, some had the ability and determination to put their memories of the war on paper; and what stories they were! As a young fellow in the years immediately following 1945, I spent countless hours reading of the heroic exploits of such military aviators as Douglas Bader, Guy Gibson, Buzz Beurling, Johnnie Johnston and many others whose adventures in the air, as told in these wonderful books, induced me to seek a career in the Royal Canadian Air Force soon after my eighteenth birthday.

Reading this, John Gardam's latest book, has left me with the same sense of awe and respect as I felt then for those who fought the war. Of course, the passage of time has had its effect on the telling. When the veterans who are the centrepiece of this collection tell their own stories, there is a modesty, a mellowness, that comes, I suspect, from fifty years of reflection upon the dramatic events that left such a mark on their young lives. There is no boasting here, no vaunting of one's exploits in the face of the enemy. On the contrary, there is a common thread of self-effacement in these stories that doesn't quite mask the quiet courage that was the hallmark of Canadian servicemen and women in World War Two.

LGeneral Paul Manson, Assistant Deputy Minister (Personnel) accepts a cheque for The Gardam Trust (fund for service people in finacial distress) from John Gardam, Assistant Secretary General, Canadian Agency, Commonwealth War Games Commission. Ottawa, Ont. December 1985
CF Photo

With one or two exceptions, the subjects of this book are what you might call ordinary people. Not all were front line types. But they all had a part to play in bringing victory, and they did it with pride and a great sense of duty. I am honoured to know several of them personally, yet in almost all cases I was unaware of the remarkable wartime experiences described in these pages.

John Gardam deserves great credit for having brought together in this volume a few stories of what it was really like in the dark days of the war. He has, as much as possible, let those who were there tell it in their own words, while himself tying it all together skillfully and sensitively.

In another fifty years, the Second World War will be deeply embedded in history. Those who took part will have passed from the scene. Time will have had another five decades to further cloud society's collective memory and understanding of the personal side of things. We should be thankful that this little volume will carry the torch, so to speak, to the young people of the year 2040. May they read it and reflect upon the futility and horror of war. May they also recognize that, in the midst of the terrible war described in <u>Fifty Years After</u>, some ordinary Canadians did some extraordinary things to change the course of history for the better.

Vice Admiral J.A. Fulton, CMM, CD

Fifty Years After is different from other histories that I have read on the Royal Canadian Navy and its part in the events of the Second World War. What makes this collation of history live are the reminiscences of the now-aging veterans who served Canada in and among the far distant ships.

Vice Admiral J.A. Fulton, Commander Marine Command, presents Colonel J. Gardam with a *BRAVO ZULU* (Well Done) certificate, Halifax, N.S. 14 July 1982
CF Photo

These are the stories that came from the lower decks, from the men at the working and action stations who portray events in factual terms often missed by historians in their detached study of war at sea.

Some of the stories, like those of Chief Petty Officer Stone in HMCS Huron and Able Seaman Dunlop in HMCS Sioux, I had heard before. The others were new to me and each enriched my understanding of the young men who volunteered for naval service. The record of their humour under adversity and memories of the pain and sorrow of matters gone wrong, over comrades lost, is enhanced by the telling. Fifty Years After is a reflection on human nature undaunted.

I am glad that Colonel Gardam included the merchant navy in this history. Too often, the merchant men are forgotten. Their ships were the prime target of Nazi U-boats, aircraft and surface raiders, and the British merchant marine - which included Canadian merchant ships and men - lost more than 100,000 officers and crew between 1939 and 1945. So many have no grave to mark. How could you forget?

Colonel Gardam is to be congratulated for his initiative in finding and interviewing so many veterans of all three services and recording their experiences of the Second World War.

Author's Preface

My first attempt to use oral history as a means of recording veteran's stories resulted in **Seventy Years After 1914-1984**. As I interviewed, recorded, researched and wrote, it became obvious I was almost too late to preserve stories from the First World War. There is but one person from that book, Jack Stotesbury, who was still alive in 1989.

My personal involvement with the people in this book has been over many years, through fleeting interviews and in some cases through a third party. General E.L.M. Burns is the only First and Second World War veteran who appears in both my oral history books.

Fifty Years After separates the stories of the Royal Canadian Navy, Canadian Army and the Royal Canadian Air Force. Each account has been checked against official histories, and in most cases by the staff of the Directorate of History in the Department of National Defence.

My one regret is that I waited so long to write this book. Too many wonderful stories escaped me because the veteran passed away suddenly. Such people as Pierre Chasse who worked with the French underground, John Simms who was a platoon commander at Anzio with the Special Service Force, and Wilfred Rushton who was serving aboard *HMCS Teme* on 29 March 1945, when she was torpedoed.

A phenomenon I did not discover when writing about the First World War was that many Second World War veterans did not want to talk about their experiences. Maybe the memory of war is still fresh in their minds and it was just too painful to talk about. As Martin Gilberts said in **Second World War**, "The greatest unfinished business of the Second World War is pain."

Fifty Years After

This book is my tribute to veterans. It contains but a microcosm of the experiences of Canadian men and women of the Second World War era. Each account but one is the story of a young person who left home to go off to war, and went willingly to do his or her best.

I am grateful to **Reader's Digest** for allowing me to use the drawings from **Tools of War**. Much of the Second World War material can be found in museums or in pictures in military history books.

It is my hope that these stories will be read by old and young alike, but particularly by the young. Young Canadians will benefit from learning of their history, when Canada went to war to preserve freedom, democracy and our unique Canadian way of life.

Chapter One

World War Two: How did it all begin?

We all longed for peace -- everybody. Some longed so deeply that they came to believe that never again would there be war.
Angus L. Macdonald

Canada fought the First Great War at a cost of 64,772 dead. Sailors, soldiers and airmen died in that war to end all wars. How could yet another world war begin just 20 years later? A complete answer takes more discussion than this book allows. Here is but a highlight of the political situation, Canada's military preparedness and the response of Canadians as, once again, they went to defend their nation.

The League of Nations covenant under Article X required that signatories join in mutual security to protect each other, even to the point of war. It was a contentious article for Prime Minister William Lyon Mackenzie King, for he "would never allow the League to draw Canada into war". The King government's fear of war was of such magnitude that the Liberals in 1930 refused to build up Canada's arsenal, declaring they were not merchants of death.

Three years later, in 1933, Hitler came to power in Germany. Within another three years, he had renounced the Treaty of Versailles, reinstated conscription and started building the mighty German navy. In 1935, Italy invaded Ethiopia. The Canadian delegate at the League of Nations -- W.R. Riddel -- proposed sanctions against Mussolini's government. Afraid Quebec's large population of Catholics would object to such sanctions, King withdrew his support from Riddel's initiative. The League was losing its power, if indeed it ever truly had any. Germany went on the march.

Six years after Hitler came to power, Germany invaded first Czechoslovakia, then Poland. It was hard to believe such military power had been amassed so quickly.

France and Britain declared war on Germany 3 September 1939, but Canada waited until after parliament was recalled 7 September. The speech from the Throne outlined "immediate participation in the war". The debate on the speech ended and the position was adopted 9 September. The next day, the proclamation was published in a special issue of the Canada Gazette. Canada's week of neutrality had ended. For the second time in a generation, Canada and Germany were at war.

With war declared, Mackenzie King spoke out dramatically on its necessity:

> It is this reliance upon force, this lust for conquest, this determination to dominate throughout the world, which is the real cause of war that threatens the freedom of mankind. Everything which free men value and cherish, on this side of the grave, is in peril.

Yet Canadians were perhaps less certain of the cause. English Canadians and French Canadians viewed the war with markedly different attitudes. The English-speaking majority were critical of Neville Chamberlain, the British prime minister, for his ineffectual attempts at peacemaking. The francophones were even more bitter, believing Canada was fighting another country's battles when she should concern herself only with defending her own shores. "Why is Canada at war? Because Britain is at war, and solely for that reason. Certainly she also [fights] for a humane cause, against German ambitions and Nazi racism, but those motives [are] not decisive." Small wonder a conscription crisis occurred four years later.

The nation responded ... but with a fervour different from that of 1914. There was no jingoism, no widespread outpouring of patriotism. As Reg Roy wrote, "The nation accepted the need for war in a sombre mood." That is not to say certain individuals did not go to great lengths to join their "own" regiment. One fellow wired Belleville, "Returning first train east. Hold a place."

Young and not so young joined up to go to sea, to learn to fly, or to become soldiers. Each had a personal reason for joining; for many it would be their first time away from home, their very first job. "On no man was there a compulsion, save that which came from his own heart," wrote Farley Mowat in **The Regiment**.

At the working level in the Royal Canadian Navy (RCN), Canadian Army and Royal Canadian Air Force (RCAF), the tiny Regular Force and the Reserves met the challenge of war with professional pride. On 26 August, the RCN received the code word FUNNEL, bringing all merchant shipping under the authority of the RCN. In Vancouver on 31 August, *HMCS Fraser* and *St Laurent* were in port holding civic celebrations when a halt to proceedings was ordered. The ships were doing 25 knots for the Panama Canal and Halifax just two hours later. By 15 September they were in Halifax, and one day later *St Laurent* sailed as part of the escort for the first convoy, HX1, to the United Kingdom. The senior service had wasted no time going to war.

The RCAF was critically short of battleworthy aircraft. On 24 August, Air Commodore Stedman went to Washington, D.C., on a shopping expedition for more aircraft. Two days later, despite the lack of aircraft, the RCAF began moving to war stations; three squadrons were posted to the Atlantic coast and one was sent to St Hubert, Quebec.

The Canadian Army also began its deployment plans early. On 24 June, proposals for concentrating units were issued. On 25 August, all Regular Force leave was cancelled, and Vital Points were under armed guard that same day. The Adjutant General telegraphed the mobilization order across Canada on 1 September.

The results at the end of the telegraph line at two infantry regiments illustrates that though few in number and ill equipped, they were still ready to be mobilized for war.

In Victoria, British Columbia, the Orderly Room Sergeant of the Canadian Scottish Regiment read the telegram and immediately called the Adjutant, Captain Parker. Parker took the telegram and hastened to the bank in downtown Victoria where the regiment's commanding officer worked as a teller. The bank was busy that Friday morning, so Parker stepped into the queue and waited his turn for the wicket.

Finally, he slid the telegram across the counter. It must have been as electrifying as a hold-up note!

At the Hastings and Prince Edward Regiment, Belleville, Ontario, "it was nearly noon when the telegraph boy rode his bicycle down the main street of the town" -- an image of small-town unhurriedness soon to be destroyed by the urgency of war. The news passed from farm, to sawmill, to mine. Tools were put down as the men rushed to the Armoury ready to do what they had trained for as members of the "Hasty Pees".

Was Canada equipped for war? No. Except for some rifles and ammunition left over from World War I, Canada was unequipped. Not one modern anti-aircraft gun did she have for the army, nor any aerial bombs for the airforce. If the artillery fired its outdated field guns, the entire ammunition supply would last just 90 minutes. The only item in large supply was harness for horses. No troops were ready for action. The RCN had six destroyers, five minesweepers and a strength of 145 officers and 1674 men. Low in personnel and equipment, the RCAF was in no better condition.

Why were things in such grim shape in 1939? The country had known since 1935 the League would not provide protection. Historian C.P. Stacey theorized that "peacetime ideas of economy and treasury control were dominant, and the war program was tailored to the domestic situation rather than the menace posed by Germany." Luckily for Canada, there were those in the Regular Force and the Reserves who kept the fires going, even when it meant using their own meagre funds.

The Treaty of Versailles stopped the fighting in November 1918, but it did not stop Germany's desire for a place in the sun, an empire. 1939-1945 was once again to be the war to end all wars. The Second World War was inevitable. As Desmond Morton wrote, "Few Canadians in the 1920s realized that the Armistice in 1918 would be no more than a truce."

Chapter Two

The Royal Canadian Navy
(Five RCN sailors and a Merchant Navy radio officer)

In September 1939 Canada's Navy went to war with 13 ships and 3000 officers and men. Six years later the numbers had risen to 373 ships and over 90,000 men and women. Canadians served throughout the world as individual members in Royal Navy ships, as well as with Allied navies. The one area where the RCN slowly assumed greater control was in the North Atlantic: by 1942 close to 200 ships and 16,000 men were providing almost half of the surface escort ships for convoys from North America to Britain. The RCAF also provided eight squadrons of Maritime patrol aircraft.

The threat of the German U-Boat grew from less than 30 submarines in 1939 to almost 500 by March 1945. Technological advances with the acoustic torpedo and the schnorkel allowed the underwater enemy to remain effective until the war ended.

Life aboard ship during the winter storms was one of constant wet, of food almost unfit to eat and of ships that were not built to take the punishment. The saying from Nelson's day of "wooden ships and iron men" applied to our sailors. The corvettes, the little vessels that Winston Churchill called "cheap but nasties" were the mainstay of Canada's Navy.

Stories in this chapter cover the big ships, corvettes and minesweepers. The war against the U-Boat in the St Lawrence was the only real enemy threat to Canada in the entire war. One Merchant Navy sailor is included: their stories are often overlooked, yet Merchant losses were just as tragic as those of the RCN.

Sea battle in the English Channel

A "not so young sailor" gave me the details of this story about a Tribal Class destroyer -- *HMCS Huron* -- and an incident that took place in the English Channel just after D-Day. The German Navy was trying to hamper the cross-channel flow of Allied craft and to reinforce and resupply the German-held port of Cherbourgh. An enemy force attacked four ships of the 19th Division -- *HMS Tartar*, flagship of Captain Basil Jones, DSO, DSC, RN; *HMS Ashanti*; *Haida* and *HMCS Huron*. It was in *Huron* that Chief Petty Officer (CPO) Len Stone was serving as the CPO Telecommunications (CPO/Tel). The enemy force of four destroyers had double the number of torpedo tubes and greater speed. Captain Jones wrote, "I came to the conclusion that it was quite necessary to press on into the enemy ... to bring about a decisive result."

Once battle was joined, *Tartar* had to give the orders to the other three ships plus keep Headquarters in Plymouth informed. Imagine the blow when:

> Four shells went upon *Tartar*'s bridge, starting a fire abaft her bridge, cutting leads [cables] to her directors [fire control mechanisms to her guns], bringing down the trellis foremast and all radar, and cutting torpedo communications to aft. The wheelhouse was also hit.

Tartar rapidly lost steam pressure. Her speed was reduced to ten knots.

Aboard *Huron*, CPO/Tel Stone observed the damage and knew *Tartar* would have difficulty communicating with the other ships, "so I went in the radio office and took over the Action Bay to see just what would happen." Len's training made him automatically take control of all radio transmissions as soon as he realized the extent of *Tartar*'s radio problems. His story continues:

> On *Tartar*'s first transmission I allowed five seconds for *Haida* to answer, and as she hadn't heard the *Tartar*'s radio message I immediately repeated [it], whereupon all the other ships

answered so I knew everything was OK. I continued to repeat *Tartar*'s radio traffic for the rest of the night.

Len's messages on ship position, speed and even *Tartar*'s action reports were all received in Plymouth. Plymouth and Captain Jones were never out of touch with the flotilla and Captain Jones "did not have to change command to another ship despite the damage his ship had suffered."

The CPO/Tel in *Tartar* realized the CPO/Tel in *Huron* was carrying the responsibility for all radio traffic, and said to Captain Jones, "*Huron* has saved the day." Not until then, with the battle over, did Jones realize how seriously damaged was his radio transmitting capability. He immediately sent a signal to *Huron's* captain: "Report on board with your Action Bay log." The record had every transmission logged by exact time; it was positive proof of Len Stone's devotion to his place of duty.

CPO Stone received a Distinguished Service Medal for his actions that day. As Len said: "Battles are fought from the ship's bridge, but they are not always aware of what goes on in the radio room, unless a signal is missed and then all hell breaks loose."

Len Stone had enlisted in the RCN in 1926 and joined *Huron* when she was commissioned in July 1943. He died while attending a *Huron* reunion in June 1987.

CPO Len Stone and his wife Sylvia after the 1945 investiture at Halifax, N.S.

Engine Room -- Ready!

Sam Brunette joined the RCN in March 1944 as a skilled machinist, he was able to join as a Petty Officer 1st Class. He did little basic training and was soon familiar with the engine room of a corvette, his trade that of Engine Room Artificer (ERA).

HMCS Lunenburg had returned to Halifax after a hectic session in both the North African landing (Torch) and D-Day (Neptune). Sam joined the *Lunenberg* when she was in refit in Saint John, New Brunswick. The ship was ready to sail on 25 December 1944 for Bermuda, where the crew was worked up with both Royal Navy and United States Navy ships. Sam remarked, "The only true excitement was when a US submarine surfaced under our keel."

One occasion remains clear in the former ERA's mind, that of one of their own depth charges being set too shallow. It resulted in an explosion heaving the stern plates and *Lunenberg* having to limp back to Plymouth for repairs. "The noise in the engine room was so loud we thought we had been hit by a torpedo," Sam said. "We seldom knew what was happening once 'Action Stations' was called." The engine room staff had to be ready for changes in speed at a moment's notice. There was no margin for error, no second chance to correct mistakes.

When *HMCS Lunenburg* was decommissioned in Sydney, Nova Scotia, the town of Lunenburg had a big party for the crew, an event of both joy and sadness as a good ship was stripped of her weapons and left tied to a jetty. Sam's memory of funny times produced this yarn about Lt Frost bringing a case of beer aboard *Lunenberg* and then telling the sailors that they had to drink it in an hour before anyone caught them with it. Said Sam, "We did not disappoint him!"

Like so many others, Sam volunteered for the Pacific when the war in Europe ended. He was sent on leave and was told to join the cruiser *HMCS Ontario* when he returned; however, the war ended before he could get to his new ship.

Sam left the RCN in January 1946 and returned to Windsor, Ontario, where he still lives. He worked for GM Cadillac Division for 23 years, retiring in December 1983.

Sam Brunette

The CAT may have saved her

Gerry Pocock joined the RCN at the age of 18. He was the youngest of five, with two brothers in the Canadian Army and a brother and sister in the RCAF. "To get away from all that", in 1943 he decided to join the Navy. After completing his basic training at Cornwallis he entered the asdic trade (locating submarines under the water), in which he was trained to detect underwater targets, because he "had excellent hearing". On arrival in Halifax, while there were two shore establishments *HMCS Peregrine* (known by the sailors as "Pretty Grim") and *Stadacona*, he was drafted aboard *Clayoquot*, a Bangor minesweeper J74. She had spent a good deal of time at sea, a "scruffy old ship who had lots of sea time behind her". Gerry said that while he was aboard "we never swept a mine, but rather acted as a surface escort on the Triangle Run -- from Halifax to Boston, to Bermuda and return." Ordinary Seaman Pocock only served aboard for four months when he was sent ashore to Cornwallis to be assessed for the Commissioned Warrant Officers course. It was November when Gerry started his training and little did he know that his time ashore was to save him from being aboard *HMCS Clayoquot* when she was torpedoed.

In Far Distant Ships Joseph Schull wrote:

In December [1944] U-boats attacked with even more reckless daring. On the 21st a Liberty ship *SS Samtucky* was torpedoed from a convoy forming up from Halifax. Three days later in the same area [on 24 December] the Bangor minesweeper *Clayoquot* was sunk with the loss of eight lives [by U806 -- Hornbostel]. The corvettes *Fennel* and *Transcona*, which were in company with her, each exploded an acoustic torpedo in its cat gear, but made no contact with the submarine.

The cat gear was a simple device of a long cable trailed behind the ship's stern. At the end were two pieces of steel that slapped together. The torpedo would be attracted to the cat sooner than the ship's screw. Gerry said they used to sing "Buffer won't you put the cat out tonight and we will sail by the light of the moon."

24

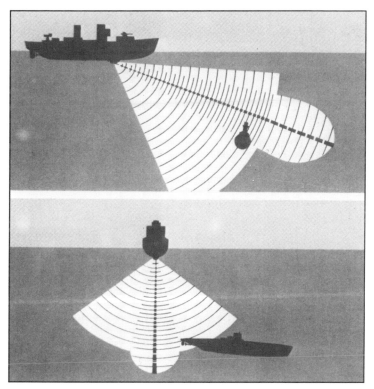

Asdic

The asdic underwater listening device got its name from the Allied Submarine Detection Investigation Committee which developed the first model during World War 1. Asdic consisted of a transmitter-receiver that sent sound impulses through the water. If the sound waves hit a submerged U-boat the echoes bounced back to the asdic receiver. The time taken for the signals to go out and the echoes to return was calculated to give the U-boat's range - the shorter the time, the closer the target. By plotting the changing ranges, the escort could track the U-boat's course.

Asdic signals were transmitted from a dome under the ship. Three impulse waves were sent out: the wide beam swept in slow stages around the ship to seek out the U-boat; the other beams fixed the U-boat's position accurately once it was located. Asdic could normally detect a U-boat at 1500 yards and track it accurately to within about 200 yards.

From **The Tools of War 1939/45**
1969 The Reader's Digest Association (Canada) Ltd. Montreal
Reproduced with permission

Able Seaman Pocock was not selected for officer training and was instead drafted overseas to join *HMCS Uganda*. The day they sailed from Halifax "we heard that President Roosevelt had died. It sent shock waves through us all."

Uganda had sailed by the time Gerry arrived, so he and eleven others were put to work decommissioning *HMCS Mayflower*, which was the first RCN corvette to cross the Atlantic (5 September 1940). He said, "What a pity we did not keep her, as she was a part of our naval history."

All these years later, Gerry and his shipmates put together what happened that fateful day before Christmas 1944. "LCdr Craig Campbell, our CO, did not deploy *Clayoquot*'s cat gear for some reason and the German torpedo struck the ship in the engine room, then the magazine blew. She began sinking fast. Many of the bulkheads had been stove in, jamming hatches, trapping people below. One of the sailors, Jones from Montreal, made most of the depth charges 'safe' before stepping into the water as the ship sank."

In Michael Hadley's **U-Boats Against Canada**, he describes how the two blasts pushed the "whole stern section into a vertical position against the hatch of the after officer's cabin." Losses were not as great as they might have been, for "the majority of the ship's company had mustered up forward for their daily issue of grog."

The ship's joker, Alex Batt, tried to cheer up his shipmates while they waited to be rescued by saying, "Flash! Canadian Minesweeper Destroys German Torpedo!" The whole event from torpedo explosion to the ship disappearing beneath the surface of the ocean took just nine minutes.

Gerry left the Navy at war's end, and from 1946 to 1949 attended the University of Toronto. He was ordained a Roman Catholic priest in 1957. He is now in his 33rd year as a priest, serving in the Ottawa area.

Bangor class minesweeper *Clayoquot*, **sunk off Halifax in December 1944**

Serving in the Sioux

Able Seamen Gordon "Mac" Dunlop of Ottawa joined the Royal Canadian Navy in January 1943 at the age of 18. He took his basic training at the RCN Training Depot, Cornwallis, Nova Scotia, and then left for gunnery training at Whale Island in Britain. Mac's first and only ship was the destroyer *HMCS Sioux*.

Sioux was equipped with 4.7-inch guns, 40-mm Bofors anti-aircraft guns and other smaller weapons. At 2,500 tons and 363 feet long, she could travel full speed at 30 knots. *Sioux* had been named *HMS Vixen* before she was commissioned 21 February 1944 under the command of LCdr Eric Boak in the Isle of Wight. *HMCS Sioux* was involved in four major operations: providing destroyer screens off the Norwegian coast; five convoy escorts to Murmansk, Russia; fire support on D-Day, 6 June 1944; and, finally the evacuation of Soroya Island at the far northern fringes of the Scandinavian Peninsula. Mac was with her for every action.

Mac's memories of the convoys to Russia dwell not on the war, but rather on the unusual aspects of that part of the world. More often than not, *Sioux's* enemy was not a German vessel but rough seas with waves 40 to 50 feet high.

The water splashing over the ship would quickly build into thick layers of ice that had to be chopped from the superstructure. Mac remembers being warned not to whistle while in Russian ports, and he also recalls playing -- and losing -- ice hockey with a *Sioux* team against the Russians.

D-Day was another memorable day. *Sioux* was "among the 78 fleets [destroyers] which opened fire ..." In **Far Distant Ships**, Joseph Schull tells of *Sioux's* role: "*Sioux's* opening target was two large buildings, each sheltering a 75-mm gun, a mile and a half to the east of St. Aubin. Within twenty minutes both guns had been silenced."

An event of the next day, 7 June, proved that even under strain the men of the RN and RCN didn't lose their sense of humour. The cruiser *HMS Belfast* decided to engage a shore target that had been assigned to the more lightly armed destroyer *Sioux*. Accordingly, *Belfast* also took over the services of *Sioux's* Forward Observation Officer (FOO). As Schull describes it, "A mild protest crossed the water from *Sioux's* signal lamp: 'Thou shalt not covet thy neighbour's FOO.' *Belfast* replied, as she fired her first salvo: 'Many are called, but FOO are chosen!'"

"Mac" Dunlop, age 18 -- Ottawa

Before leaving for Scapa Flow in June, *Sioux* engaged enemy troops at the mouth of the River Orne and also shelled a battery of German field artillery. Young gunner Mac Dunlop was putting his Whale Island training to full use! On 24 June Mac was part of a whaler crew that pulled a young Royal Navy sailor from the English Channel. Eric Le Tessier was in *HMS Swift* when she sank on 24 June. (Mac and Eric did not meet again until 44 years later, in Ottawa.)

In February 1945 Mac sailed to Russia for the fourth time. Schull recounts the story of the journey:

> *Sioux* was en route to Murmansk with a convoy which had to fight its way north through foul weather and a series of attacks by German torpedo bombers. ... On the 10th of February one plane [Junkers 88] swept down to launch a torpedo ... [at *Sioux*]. The destroyer had to take drastic avoiding action; but as she swerved aside she saw her anti-aircraft fire registering on the German.

Four days later, on 14 February, *Sioux* and *HMS Zambezi* and *Zest* were ordered to Soroya Island. In just three and a half hours they took on all 500 inhabitants of the island. Soon afterward the civilians were transferred to merchant ships and returned to England.

Mac's stay at Scapa Flow was brief. On 12 March, *Sioux* sailed again for Murmansk, and this time "the convoy was met by a force of U-Boats" which sank three ships. *Sioux* returned to Scotland for the last time. She sailed home for Halifax on 6 April 1945.

Mac Dunlop left the Navy when he was just 20 years old. He is now retired and lives in Ottawa.

She ain't no wreck

Ed Slater had just turned 18 when he joined the RCNVR in October 1940. Like so many young men, Ed had never had a real job before. He took basic training in Vancouver and Victoria, but his engine room training was done at Comox, British Columbia. After that he went through a long period of waiting. The day Pearl Harbor was bombed -- 7 December 1941 -- Ed and his pals were assigned to walk the Victoria beach with .303 rifles, but no ammunition: Fear of invasion caused some strange decisions!

In January 1942, Ed was sent to Halifax but was still not assigned to a ship. With 14 others, he volunteered for a special job and found himself en route to New York City. In New York they joined an RN cruiser that was in the Brooklyn Yard for repairs. When the ship sailed in May, the Canadians remained aboard and went to England. *HMCS Niobe* in Scotland was Ed's next assignment, a training establishment where he worked in the laundry. He was glad to leave the suds behind when he was sent to Londonderry, Ireland, in July. One evening an RN Petty Officer asked "Are you a stoker?" Ed's affirmative answer resulted in, "You are needed aboard an RN ship at once."

Ed's first, but not last assignment to an RN ship was *HMS Venomous*. A storm made Ed so seasick that he remembers little of the trip to Iceland. The destroyer was to escort a convoy to Russia, but the boilers gave out and it was back to Londonderry and another RN ship, the Hunt Class destroyer *HMS Zetland* of the Londonderry Special Escort Division. This meant action for Ed in the Atlantic escorting convoys to and from America.

On 4 September 1942 they escorted *RMS Queen Elizabeth* loaded with US troops en route to England. When the *Zetland* sailed on 28 October it was to take part in Operation Torch, the invasion of North Africa. On 8 November, *HMS Zetland* was part of the patrol off "Charlie" Beach, the landing at Algiers. The *Zetland* fired on the fort at Cape Matifu and put the guns out of action. When *HMS Broke* was damaged, the *Zetland* took her in tow, but due to heavy weather the two ships collided; the *Broke* sank, and *Zetland* had to rescue her crew.

31

On 30 January 1943, *HMS Zetland* once again rescued a crew, this time from *HMS Samphire*, which had been sunk by a U-Boat. Air attack damage and the collision with *HMS Broke* required *Zetland* to return to Plymouth for repairs.

At long last Ed was able to rejoin the RCN. On 3 June he travelled north to Scotland and *HMCS Niobe*, wearing an HMS cap tally and no Canada flashes! A short course to qualify as a Petty Officer followed, and then Ed returned to Esquimalt, British Columbia where he joined a ship that had just been launched, K317 *HMCS Chebogue*.

HMCS Chebogue was commissioned on 22 February, 1944, worked up in local waters and then sailed through the Panama Canal for Halifax, arriving in April. The ship was supposed to be called *Yarmouth*, but as there was already a British ship by that name, she was named after a river and village near Yarmouth, Nova Scotia. K317 visited Yarmouth in mid-June before sailing on her first convoy escort, HXF 296; no merchant ships were lost. In early October, *Chebogue* sailed as Senior Officer's Ship of convoy EG C-1. The enemy struck on 4 October 1944.

A U-Boat was sighted at about 1100 hours some 20 to 30 miles from the convoy. "Surface Alert" was sounded. Ed, who had just come off watch in the engine room, went to his station in charge of the ammunition party at the forward gun. Later that evening the Captain, LCdr Maurice F. Oliver, went up the mast to join the lookout. He "saw the only U-Boat I had seen in the war with my own eyes." It was 13,000 yards away on the surface. Star shells lit up the evening sky; the chase was on!

The U-Boat was U1227 (Altmyer). The submarine's log tells the story:

> 2250 hrs. Range taken by my radar; continued on the surface. Enemy [*Chebogue*] using star shells, escort approaching fast. Dived after firing torpedo; do not expect a hit as torpedoes unreliable and the escort has its CAT [antitorpedo gear] deployed. Six minutes later an explosion, a hit? Sounds of depth charges or breaking up. 2350 hrs. Return to periscope depth, escort stopped, we have a hit!

HMCS Chebogue took this torpedo in the stern. Six crewmen died instantly. Of the eight other men wounded, one more was to die. The rest of the crew scrambled to control the damage and treat the wounded. Then they waited for help. It was two long hours before *HMCS Gifford*, a ship that had rescued the crew of *HMCS Valleyfield* earlier that year, came alongside. *HMCS Arnprior* and *Chambly* were close behind. *Gifford* was signalling *Chambly* to "carry out anti-submarine search in area of the wreck" when *Chebogue*'s captain interrupted, "We ain't no wreck." While the wounded were being transferred to one of the

Ed Slater in 1944 on joining *HMCS Chebogue* **(ensign rank shows)**

other ships, LCdr Oliver asked for 30 volunteers to remain with *Chebogue* while she was towed to harbour in England. Every man volunteered. LCdr Oliver chose just 37 to remain; the rest were transferred to other ships. It was 11 October before landfall was sighted by the crew taking the *Chebogue* to England. Ill fortune struck again, for a sudden storm sent the *Chebogue* aground and the crew had to abandon ship. The next day she was refloated and the weary crew took her alongside in Port Talbot.

Meanwhile, Ed arrived in St- John's, Newfoundland, aboard the *Chambly*. After a few days he flew to Halifax, and was back in Vancouver by 19 October for survivor's leave. He returned to Halifax for a shore posting in *HMCS Dockyard*. Poor health plagued him, and in no time tuberculosis was diagnosed. Ed was in hospital on VE-Day, the day of the infamous Halifax riots. He was moved to the "San" in Vancouver, where he stayed until August 1945 when he was discharged from the RCN. He was not cured of tuberculosis until March 1946.

Unable to return to manual work, Ed Slater trained as a bookkeeper. In 1948 Ed went to work for the Royal Canadian Legion. His Legion work ended over 40 years later when he retired from Dominion Command as the Secretary, Veterans Services Committee. He is now retired and living in Manotick, Ontario. (Special Note: Ed loaned me the video *She Ain't No Wreck*, which was a most exceptional source of information.)

First Ship

'Twas in the month of October, when the Huns were out in force,
Across the North Atlantic, the Captain set our course.
"We're headed for Newfoundland boys, this convoy must go through,
Those merchant ships and men on board, their safety lies with you."
We bade farewell to Irish shores as oft we'd done before,
Never dreaming as we left that land that we'd ne'r see her more.
With signal lamps all blazing and our ensign flying free,
The ships took up position and headed out to sea.
The striking force was ordered back and we were left alone,
To guard some sixty merchant ships and bring them safely home.
Not a man among the crew nor the Captain of our ship,
Had ever thought that this would be our last and final trip.
For in the mid Atlantic a lurking U-Boat lay,
It was ready and was waiting till a convoy passed that way.
That sub was finally spotted by a lookout on the mast,
The crew was called to action, we had found that sub at last.
Warships protect the merchant ships like a bear protects its cubs,
So we moved into position between the convoy and the sub.

The sub well knew the danger and quietly slipped away,
The four ships of our escort group searched in vain that day.
Then under the cover of darkness the sub rose to surface once more,
It was quickly seen on our radar screen followed by our big guns roar.
Those shells were bursting round her as she was forced below,
The sub fired one torpedo that was meant for the *Chebogue*.
Chebogue was struck a mortal blow as she closed in for the kill,
The die was cast, one mighty blast, and everything went still.
Sadly we abandoned her, there was nothing we could do,
'Twas but the price that must be paid so the convoy could get through.
May we all remember her proudly, lady of the sea,
Remember too the men who died to keep our nation free.
Chebogue is your adopted ship; Yarmouth is her home,
May she always be remembered as the ship you call your own.

Able Seaman Frank Murphy
(Written October 1945 -- St. John's, Newfoundland)

HMCS Chebogue **under tow after torpedo attack 4 Oct 1944**

Under the Red Ensign

My first meeting with Gordon Olmstead was in the summer of 1989 when he was preparing a submission to Parliament concerning Canadian Merchant Navy seamen who died in the Second World War. His wartime story is unique, for although he spent most of his service as a prisoner of war, he still continues a very special relationship with his wartime comrades.

Gordon was born in the Prairies, and by 1939 he had his Second Class Wireless Operator's licence from the Radio College of Canada. He went to join the Royal Canadian Corps of Signals, but when told the job he would be doing was in Winnipeg he decided to seek action at sea. As a Marconi Company operator Gordon went to New York to join his first merchant ship, the motor vessel *Agnita*, a sulphuric acid carrier. When she was not loaded with sulphuric acid, she carried oil.

Gordon's first voyage to South America was followed by a trip to Freetown, "a major convoy port in West Africa". After discharging her cargo, it was back to America with a full hold of oil. Only a few days en route the *Agnita* sighted a large ship. It was the German armed merchant raider the *Kormoran*, armed with six 5.9-inch guns. Sadly, the *Agnita's* 4-inch and 12-pounder armament meant suicide if they tried to fight, and since they could not outrun the Germans, "We gave up!"

Gordon and the crew took to the boats, ready to set sail for the West Indies. Captain Stan Algar was taken by the Germans, who sent him back for the rest of his crew -- they were all to be prisoners of war. Quickly the crew were taken aboard *Kormoran*. A German demolition team put explosive charges in the engine room of the *Agnita*. There was a large explosion, but *Agnita* just sat there; her buoyancy was such that torpedoes and gunfire had to be used before she would sink. About two weeks later Gordon and the rest of the crew members were on deck when they came upon another German raider, *Nordmark*. The two raiders were to refuel U105 and U106. Gordon watched as torpedoes were taken from the mother ships and stowed aboard the U-Boats.

Gordon Olmstead's identification photo, used at the Milag

Landfall was Bordeaux, France. The merchant seamen were placed in a prison camp nearby for nine days. They were then put in a railway box car for a five-day trip to a prisoner-of-war camp near Bremen, Germany. In October 1941 Gordon was marched to Milag (a prisoner-of-war camp for merchant seamen), where he was to remain for three and a half years.

On 28 April 1945 the British Army, Guards Armoured Division, freed the prisoners in Milag. Gordon was flown to England early in May and reported to Liverpool. After 11 days at sea aboard the *Bayano* he arrived in Halifax. Gordon recalls, "We had no uniforms and were not permitted service fares on the railroad." This unjust treatment of the Merchant Navy was an indication of the policy that did not accord veterans' preference to those who sailed "under the Red Ensign".

As recently as March 1988, Veterans Affairs wrote to Gordon "that for legislative purposes merchant seamen are identified as civilians, not veterans" (and benefits for civilians are not the same as benefits for Armed Forces veterans). This decision means that the 10,500 merchant seamen -- whose casualty rates were one in four in the Battle of the Atlantic -- are not entitled to the same benefits as wartime members of the RCN, Canadian Army and RCAF. Gordon continues the battle to gain the same benefits for his wartime comrades.

Gordon Olmstead retired from his employment with the Government of Canada in 1978. He lives in Nepean, Ontario. As President of The Canadian Merchant Navy Prisoner of War Association, Gordon continues to fight for fair recognition for wartime merchant seamen.

Chapter Three

The Canadian Army
(Eighteen soldiers and one nurse)

The Canadian Army of 1939 had a very small Permanent Force, a large Militia and equipment that was so substandard that the Army was just a paper tiger.

It was some kind of miracle that saw 7500 members of the 1st Canadian Division sail for England just three months after war was declared. The formation had men, but very little equipment and no collective training.

Then, in December 1941, the Army fought and fell at Hong Kong, once again poorly trained, with no Canadian heavy weapon support and on an island from which there was no escape.

Eight months later was the Dieppe Raid, in August 1942. Some 5000 soldiers of 2nd Division went ashore for just hours. The raid produced the largest Canadian Army losses ever, over 900 in a single day.

Another year was to pass before July 1943, when the 1st Canadian Division and the 1st Canadian Army Tank Brigade invaded Sicily. Later, the 5th Armoured Division joined them in the heavy fighting up the narrow roads of Italy, where every bridge was blown, roads were mined and static defence lines of enormous strength had to be broken. Less than six months before the end of the war the Canadians in Italy finally joined their comrades in North West Europe.

The 3rd Canadian Division [with three armoured regiments] was the only Canadian formation that took part in D-Day -- 6 June 1944.

The 2nd and 4th Divisions crossed into Normandy and the final great advance into Germany began. The clearance of the English Channel ports and the battle for the Scheldt had to be won before the crossing of the Rhine in February 1945. The Netherlands was liberated in March. East and West (Russian and United States Armies) met at the Elbe River on 25 April, and just days later, on 7 May, the war in Europe came to an end. The atomic bombs dropped on Nagasaki and Hiroshima in early August ended the Second World War.

The stories in this chapter form a mosaic of the Canadian Army at war.

A Cape Breton Highlander prepares for war

Reg Roy, a signaller with the Cape Breton Highlanders, wrote me a letter epitomizing the lack of preparedness of the Canadian Army at the outbreak of war. I reprint part of that letter here.

I joined the Cape Breton Highlanders in the summer of 1939 as a signaller. I remember taking signalling training in the early spring to get my qualification. When the war broke out, therefore, I was in the militia, 16 years old, and just about ready to enter Grade 12. The coming of the war came as no surprise -- even a 16-year-old who had lived through the late 1930s could see that Germany was expanding and sooner or later had to be stopped. In any event, I opted to join the Active Force rather than go to school. I reported to the "barracks" when word was broadcast on the local radio station, CJCB.

When we reported for duty we were issued with white spats, red and white stockings, a kilt, a sporran, a First World War tunic, a Glengarry cap and a First World War rifle and bayonet. We had not one single field vehicle -- not even a pair of roller skates. We had no trucks, no universal carriers, no jeeps, no motorcycles, not a thing. Insofar as weapons were concerned, we had no two-or three-inch mortars, no Bren light machine-guns, no anti-tank guns. We did have several First World War Lewis machine-guns, but that was all. There were no Tommy guns or Sten guns or anything of that nature. Incidentally, there were no rifle ranges nearby, and I can't remember one instance of going out on any range and firing either the rifle or Lewis machine-gun during the time we were in Cape Breton.

Since I was in the Signals Platoon, we applied ourselves with great diligence to learning everything we could with the equipment we had. Here, again, the equipment was of First World War vintage. We had several old DIII field telephones, an unlimited amount of wire to connect them, two dozen signalling flags, several Lucas lamps and four or five heliographs -- the latter probably used during the Boer War for signalling on the veldt in South Africa. A few members of the Signals Platoon (my brother, for example) were ham radio operators and knew quite a bit about wireless. However, at this time, we had no modern radio or wireless sets. About the only thing we could do, therefore, was to practise constantly with Morse code. I remember the required speed for Morse was 10 words a minute, but some of us got so proficient that we could send and receive at 25 words a minute, which is about as fast as you can write.

Our lack of military knowledge was hair-raising. We were good at foot and arms drill, we kept our rifles oiled and our bayonets gleaming, we used gallons of Blanco and silver polish on our First World War webbing, and there was a great deal of basic drill. We were taught a little bit about military history, military administration, map reading, military law, hygiene, a little bit about chemical warfare, and minor tactics. There was no area nearby set aside for company or battalion manoeuvres. The unit had a certain number of duties to perform with respect to defence. This was really group sentry duty. There were certainly no battalion schemes that I can remember -- but one must keep in mind that we didn't have a full-scale battalion and we still didn't have very many weapons. Our commanding officer, second-in-command and most of our company commanders were of First World War vintage. We had to use our imaginations when we were taught by them. They might mention grenades -- we had never seen one. They might talk about stringing barbed wire -- we didn't have any. They would try to tell us about trench mortars -- it would be quite some time before we received those. We had no instructional films -- and I suppose that's just as well because we had no film projectors. The anti-aircraft platoon of headquarters company had never seen a modern fighter; on the other hand, at that point we had no anti-aircraft weapons. From a military point of view, we were abysmally ignorant -- not because we wanted to be, but because the nation was so tremendously unprepared for war.

The Cape Breton Highlanders went overseas in the late fall of 1941. It was not until we got overseas that our unit and our Division began, slowly but surely, to become equipped with some of the guns and machines that we were going to use in warfare. However, this is another story. It was going to take quite some time before we began to learn battle drill tactics and shape ourselves into a unit that had a sufficient measure of confidence to go into battle with the expectations of success.

Reg Roy taught at Royal Roads Military College and currently is teaching at the University of Victoria, British Columbia.

Cape Breton Highlanders capture a Nazi flag in Holland in 1945; Reg Roy, far right

Two mines and you're out!

A young soldier from Toronto began his career in Camp Borden, Ontario, in August 1940. Pat Grieve joined as a trooper after being sworn in as a member of the Armoured Corps by F.F. Worthington (Worthy), Commander of the School. Along with a handful of other officers and men, Pat was to be part of the nucleus of the Armoured School. Trooper Grieve was shown how to wear his uniform (including how to blacken his brown boots), taught the technical aspects of the .50 and .303 Vickers machine-guns, and then told to instruct others.

In late 1940 a trainload of French Renault tanks arrived in Camp Borden from the United States. Worthy had purchased them (for just $120 each) as scrap metal to avoid complications with a neutral country. For each tank, Pat and the others were given four spark plugs, a can of water for the radiator and enough gasoline to start and move the tanks. Pat's tank "had bird nests in the hatches and grass growing on its tracks. [I] inserted the plugs, filled the radiator, poured in the gas and started to crank; I got my tank started." The Renaults were immediately pressed into service to teach tank tactics to the hundreds of officers and men who were waiting to be trained.

Pat accepted a commission, joined the Halifax Rifles, and left for England, where he transferred to the Canadian Grenadier Guards. Pat's regiment crossed the Normandy beaches in July 1944.

The Grenadiers had just a few hours to get sorted out before joining the other Canadian formations in the drive for Caen. The Germans knew they were being encircled and they fought hard to extricate themselves. Each mile captured by the Allies cost many human lives and machines. Meanwhile, the Polish forces fighting near Chambois were being surrounded by the Germans. The Poles could not be reinforced, or given medical aid or supplies.

On 10 August Pat left the Regimental Headquarters Troop and took command of the Reconnaissance Troop of light Stuart tanks. Eleven days later when the Grenadiers were ordered to hold the roads near Trun and Chambois, Pat's troop moved forward.

44

Ordered to find routes for the regimental tanks, Pat's troop was stopped by a large crater in an orchard. Pat got out and, after checking the area for damaged bridges and passable routes, stood on the road to direct the tanks to safety. It was just before noon, and the rain was pouring down. Suddenly there was a huge explosion under the tank; it had hit a mine. Pat was badly

Pat Grieve, England 1944

injured with "wounds to the thigh, stomach, head and eye". Luckily, the Commanding Officer arrived with a jeep ambulance, and Pat was rushed to the Regimental Aid Post. By the next day he was back in England in hospital.

Reinforcements were filling the gaps left by the wounded and killed. When I asked about the reinforcement system in vogue in 1945, Pat quickly pointed out:

> We really didn't have time for indoctrination when they arrived via the Tank Delivery Regiment. You assumed that they had been trained and you just took them into battle. Some new officers didn't seem to adapt fast enough and they were the ones who were knocked out first.

In December 1944 Pat was back in action as the Germans began their desperate attack through the Ardennes forest toward the English Channel. A few months later, on 5 April 1945, Pat and the regimental padre, John Anderson, were trying to find the graves of two Grenadiers killed while a Dutch town was being cleared of the enemy. As Pat and the padre, accompanied by two boy scouts directing them, drove toward the cemetery, there was a blinding flash and a huge explosion; they had hit a mine. A guard who had been left to stop all traffic had left his post. Once again Pat was badly injured. For Pat and the padre it was back to England and the hospital until after the war ended. The fate of the boy scouts is unknown. Two mines, and now Pat Grieve was out of the war for good.

Pat Grieve remained in the Army after the war. He served in Petawawa from October 1948 to June 1951 and again from 1959 to 1961. He commanded the Royal Canadian Dragoons, the 4th Brigade in Germany and the Canadian Land Forces Staff College in Kingston, Ontario. He retired as a Brigadier General to the position of Secretary General, Canadian Agency, Commonwealth War Graves Commission. He is now retired and living at Sharbot Lake, Ontario.

Canloan with the East Lancs

Burt Harper did not see action with a Canadian infantry regiment, but rather with the East Lancashire Regiment of the British Army as a Canloan officer.

In the fall of 1943 a scheme was devised whereby Canadian Officers could volunteer to serve with Regiments of the British Army [with] a shortage of junior officers. The Canadian Army at this time had a surplus of officers. The Canadian Government offered to loan Junior Officers to the British Army on a voluntary basis, under the code name "Canloan". They were attached for all purposes, except pay; 623 Infantry Officers together with 50 Ordnance Officers, whom the Royal Army Ordnance Corps were anxious to have serve under the scheme. While with the British each wore the cap badge of the Regiment to which he was attached, as well as the Canada flash [on the sleeve of his tunic].

Burt Harper was a lieutenant in the North Shore Regiment when he volunteered. He found himself with a special sort of unit:

My choice of the 1st Battalion East Lancashire Regiment was strictly a chance one. I made the selection from a list of infantry units of those divisions scheduled for the Normandy invasion force, presented to us aboard ship before we debarked at Liverpool in April 1944. As it happened, the unit I chose was a permanent battalion -- as opposed to territorial -- returning back from India in 1938 after a seven-year overseas tour, to France in 1939, and through Dunkirk in 1940. By Canadian standards I was relatively experienced, with four years service as an NCO and officer at that stage. Two-thirds of my British platoon, on the other hand, had at least 12 years service, including the experience of being shot at. My platoon sergeant was the typical "old school" sergeant, who had joined the Army as a boy soldier two years before I was born! Most of the lads had the very thick, broad Lancashire accent. "Pick up thy musket, Sam" and all that, thickly sprinkled with Indian

Army slang. This was a real problem for me at first, not being "bilingual". My transition from command of Canadian to British troops needed some adjustment in outlook. The British soldier, because of his background in the more disciplined English class structure, differs from the Canadian in certain fundamental ways, particularly in the approach to leadership. The British soldier accepts his officer more easily as the natural leader, and gives his loyalty and trust more readily. The officer falls naturally into his leadership role; it is not necessarily a role acquired through military service.

Unbelievable though it may sound today, Burt had never owned a bicycle, nor could he ride one. Where he had grown up in New Brunswick, bicycles were only for the better-off families. His first contact with a two-wheeled monster was a big Harley-Davidson motorcycle during his officer training. After many spills, bruises and a wrecked motorbike or so, the instructors were pleased to give Burt a passing mark, probably only to get rid of him in the expectation that he would be more danger to the enemy if he did ride one in action. But he still had no bicycle experience.

I landed in Normandy as a platoon commander on 25 June 1944. The fighting was almost two miles inland at that time, and almost immediately the battalion was ordered forward to form a firm base for an attack by another division. The CO and company commanders took off at once to go forward and make their reconnaissance [recce]. We platoon commanders were given an RV from the map where we would receive our orders and make our own recce before the troops arrived. We were to move up by bicycle because time was pressing, and our soldiers would follow on foot in a short time. I found a convenient pile of earth to stand on and boarded the bike, and a few wild gyrations and 10 yards nearer the enemy I came crashing to the ground in a tangle of equipment and hurt pride. I made two or three more attempts to take off over the rough ground and finally I grew desperate. I then ran, walked, and occasionally tried, always unsuccessfully, to mount and drive that cursed bike on my way forward over some of the most torn-up ground on the beach head. Full of foreboding, not of the enemy but of my fellow-officers' contempt, I reached the RV to find no one in sight. My heart sank. I had missed my first battle. Miracle of miracles, there came the others, riding their bikes nicely. They had been diverted by heavy shelling and had lost their way.

The official history of the East Lancashire Regiment describes another action in which Burt took part, the crossing of the Meuse — Escaut Canal by night on 15 September 1944.

The canal was about 50 yards wide. It had steep, slippery, stone-faced banks from the water's edge to about four feet up; once off the bank a man would be out of his depth suddenly and immediately. At 1600 hours the battalion moved to its assembly area one mile south of the canal and among the woods, and here it remained, resting, feeding and carrying out some "dry" boat drill until 2030 hours. Rafting stores and 16 Mark III boats arrived at 1930 hours. This allowed for five boats to each crossing site, and six for rafting. Unfortunately, the weather broke and heavy rain started to fall, and continued for the greater part of the night.

So far this piece of history has no excitement, bravery or bloodshed, but Burt's platoon was about to enter drama:

About nine p.m. we moved up to an assembly area some 600 yards from the canal, and then the long wait began. Waiting for imminent action is always trying, especially for the men in the sections, who have little to do but wait. At 2300 we moved up toward the canal, guided by white tapes laid by the Intelligence Section, and stopped at a marker 100 yards from the canal. Then the artillery began to beat a drumfire on the far bank, and as it lifted I led the first boat through the gap. Suddenly and almost unexpectedly we were at the very edge of the stone-faced, very steep and slippery canal bank, with the water about eight feet below, about twice the distance expected. Our drills hadn't catered for this! In haste I scrambled clear of the path of the fast-following boat, and

THE EAST LANCASHIRE
REGIMENT

**The badge worn by Burt
Harper as a Canloan officer**

shouted to those carrying to hold everything. I can only assume what with the noise and in the darkness they thought I was exhorting them to greater effort, because the forward motion seemed to speed up, and as each boat carrier reached the edge he had to let go or be carried into the canal below. The bow of the boat dipped down to the water and, propelled by the pushers at the rear, took on a momentum of its own. I realized that we were about to lose the boat and, in desperation, as the stern went by I leaped aboard. With this added boost and the steep slope down which it slid, the boat and I shot off into the darkness and disappeared, leaving behind a very startled platoon, no doubt marvelling at the enthusiasm of their Canadian officer. Boat and stowaway skimmed across the canal. I struggled to my feet, only to be knocked flat as it hit the enemy side -- fortunately out of sight of both friend and foe. When I did manage to grab a paddle, few athletes, Olympic or otherwise, ever expended more energy than I did in recrossing that 50 or so yards of water. I embarked my platoon, and as each one slid down the bank to the boat, I couldn't resist a few sarcastic comments about how nice it was to have them join me.

Burt Harper and five other Canadian officers with the East Lancashire Regiment crossed the Normandy beach in June 1944. Three were to be killed in action. The others, including Burt, were wounded. This high rate of battle casualty coincides with the overall Canloan statistics: killed in action or died of wounds 128 (20%); wounded 310 (50%); prisoners of war 27 (5%); total 465 (75%).

Burt Harper remained in the army post-war, eventually retiring to take up a position as a public servant in the Department of National Defence. He retired from DND in 1987 and now lives in Ottawa.

Blown out of the turret at Falaise

Bob Osborne's story fills me with sadness. **Peace in War,** his unpublished manuscript, failed to be printed because of his untimely death due to cancer less than a year after he retired from teaching Divinity at Carleton University. Bob's book "began from a packet of letters that [his] mother gave [him] one Christmas before she died". The preface described **Peace in War** as "the very stuff of which history is made". Bob's last four days of active service were the 7th to the 10th of August, 1944, when his regiment, the Canadian Grenadier Guards, took part in Phase 2 of Operation Totalize in Normandy.

Bob's narrative for 7 August is what one would expect from the wireless operator and gun loader of the Troop Commander's tank. "The tank has been gassed up and the ammunition carefully stowed in the racks. We are all thinking the same thing. Will I be alive to see the sunset tomorrow?" The padre, John Anderson, visited the tank, and the four crew members took communion. Reflecting on the 23rd Psalm's "I will fear no evil," Bob commented that the author of that Psalm had not seen "what a German 88 anti-tank gun could do to a Sherman tank". Throughout the night the tanks rumbled forward as bombers and artillery shells hit the enemy positions. Toward dawn the unit paused and the officer left for more instructions. Bob looked out at the wide plain before them: "Tanks were fanned out everywhere, but there was no enemy shooting at us." Suddenly, as the first rays of light broke over the horizon, the American aircraft started bombing. In **The Victory Campaign**, C.P. Stacey explains the appalling results. There were "gross errors on the part of two twelve-plane groups.... The areas struck, far behind the fighting line, were packed with Allied troops moving up or waiting to move up." Wrote Bob, "If they're bombing the enemy positions, then we're half way to Berlin." When the troop officer arrived back at his tank, he reported gravely, "There has been a terrible mistake; bombs have fallen among our echelons." (B vehicles used to bring forward supplies.)

It was a long day, filled with tension, but when night finally came Bob's tank crew had lived to see the sunset. At 0330 hours on 9 August,

Number 2 Squadron -- the one Bob belonged to -- was on the march again, this time with a company of the Lake Superior Regiment. The attack went in and yet another French village was cleared. Night fell again, and all too soon dawn arrived on the 10th, a day Bob was never to forget.

The Squadron commander had joined Bob's tank, meaning that they were controlling the actions of Number 2 Squadron. "The most nerve-wracking encounter that a tank man has to face is a frontal assault on a prepared [strongly defended] position." The advance began as the squadron moved out, one tank behind the other. "The early morning mist was just beginning to lift." Filled with tension, Bob grew increasingly certain of impending danger. Without warning, the leading tank was hit:

> There we stalled. What were we waiting for? Nobody seemed to know what to do next. Suddenly we were in trouble. We began to get shot at from a screen of anti-tank guns and Tiger tanks lurking in the heavily wooded area to our front. The CO called an O Group [passing of verbal orders]. The major left the tank and I got up on the commander's seat.

The enemy had watched the Grenadiers move over the crest of the hill, and then they started to destroy them one by one.

> The battle-experienced officers [ones who had fought in North Africa and Italy] now began to show their worth. Capt Curt Greenleaf was calmly walking about regrouping Number 2 Squadron to fight back. Majors Ned Amy of Number 1 Squadron and "Snuffy" Smith of Number 3 were a great steadying influence when near panic was gripping the regiment. They went from tank to tank encouraging the crews.

Bob was still commanding the lead tank, and he and his gunner were trying to locate the Tiger tank that was cutting the Grenadiers to pieces. "I can see him!" called out the gunner. Bob looked through the binoculars, and there it was, "a big 62-ton monster. He was moving his gun, swinging on us." (The German tank had a hand-operated traverse, not a powered one like the Sherman.) Bob gave the fire order: "Gunner, traverse left -- steady on, thirteen hundred [feet to the target]

The Tiger tank with its 88-mm gun and 100-mm frontal armour was a most successful tank destroyer in the German Army

From **Tools of War 1939/45**
1969 The Reader's Digest Association (Canada) Ltd. Montreal
Reproduced with permission

-- enemy tank -- FIRE!" As the round left the 17-pounder tank gun, Bob says, "In the same instant I could hear a noise like an express train -- then a sickening, rending crash as the Tiger's shell smashed into our turret."

Covered in flames, Bob was blown out of the turret. (Sherman tanks were nicknamed "Ronsons" because they flared up so easily.) Bob's words make one cringe:

I was on fire -- my clothes were almost gone -- my hair was alight. I tried to crawl away from the burning tank -- which was going up like fireworks on the 1st of July -- the grenades, phosphorous bombs, tank gun and machine-gun ammunition. What an inferno!... This was the end. I felt like I was going down a long dark tunnel. So this was what death was like -- not too bad, I thought.

Joe Arnold, the driver of another knocked-out Sherman, ran over and beat out the flames. Then he picked up the unconscious Bob and carried him from the battlefield, away from the war. The regiment lost a third of its tanks that day, and 59 crewmen were killed or wounded.

Bob Osborne was taken to Number 11 Canadian General Hospital, where the treatment for his burns and wounds lasted until November. He arrived back in Halifax on 1 December 1944. Many years later Doctor Bob Osborne and I became friends when he was teaching at Carleton University. He was a wonderful man, a great human being. I believe I am a better person because I knew him.

Transport platoon officer

Bob Jones was an officer in the Royal Canadian Army Service Corps. He joined the Army in September 1939 and trained in Gordon Head, British Columbia, and Red Deer, Alberta. After several short postings as a supply officer in Canada, he went overseas in 1943 and eventually joined the 4th Division Troops Company as a transport platoon officer. The 5th Canadian Infantry Brigade was the formation with which he was to see action in the 2nd Canadian Division.

Bob's first brush with the enemy came when he crossed the English Channel to Normandy in mid July 1944.

> We were in convoy and the ships to our front and port and astern were torpedoed by German motor torpedo boats. The sea was filled with soldiers and sailors in life jackets. We did not stop, but you could have reached out and touched them. We were told the Navy would rescue them. It was a horrifying feeling to just leave them.

Road convoy duties filled the days and nights that followed: ammunition, food and gasoline were trucked to the front; German prisoners to the rear. The one unusual cargo was hundreds of Dutch civilians, who were carried out of Antwerp when the German V-2s were targeted upon this vital port. On two occasions Bob's unit was bombed by Allied airforces by mistake. He recalls, "Two Air Observation pilots [AOPs] took their Auster aircraft up amongst the bombers, firing orange flares trying to stop the bombers." C.P. Stacey writes that 4th Division believed "one AOP plane prevented more bombs from falling", whereas ACM Harris thought these brave acts "gave misleading indicators and succeeded only in making the confusion worse". Bob still regards this as a brave act.

The day before the war ended, Bob and his driver were travelling in a jeep. Suddenly, the road blew up around them as they hit a mine. The driver was killed instantly, but Bob was blown clear of the totally destroyed vehicle -- a sad memory from so long ago.

Bob Jones

Bob remained in the post-war Army, becoming a parachutist and, in 1958, an Army pilot. His final posting was to Fort Rucker, Alabama, as a helicopter test pilot and a flying instructor. He retired from the Army in 1967 and joined the Ministry of Transport. Bob Jones is now retired and lives in Nepean, Ontario.

Kangaroo -- a new weapon

Wartime is a time for innovation -- new weapons and new ideas. One such inventive unit was the 1st Canadian Armoured Carrier Regiment -- the Kangaroos. The unit was created on the field of battle and disbanded at war's end in 1945. The only CO was Gordon Churchill, who later became a Member of Parliament and Cabinet Minister. Sgt Arnold Bannister (no relation to Roy) was also a member of the regiment.

Sgt Bannister first served with the 12th Field Regiment (Self Propelled), RCA. Their guns were "to be Priests, Sherman tank chassis mounting a 105-mm gun". Getting used to mobile artillery did not come easily to the members of a 25-pounder towed regiment. As the war diary explained:

> On January 24 [1944] Exercise Cordage began.... We fired over the infantry, ran in to and landed on the beach -- the wrong one -- and then deployed inland. Our first ranging round landed on the Winnipeg Rifles Battalion HQ and this discouraged them very quickly.

On D-Day the regiment was first Canadian artillery unit to fire -- at D+1 hours from the left of Mike Green Beach. The regiment was supporting the Regina Rifles, Canadian Scottish and Royal Winnipeg Rifles, all of the 7th Canadian Infantry Brigade.

On 24 August, Sgt Bannister left the artillery and reported to 1st Armoured Personnel Carrier Squadron. The casualties to the infantry were so high that General Simonds decided that the infantry should be carried onto the objective in armoured track vehicles. The short history of the Kangaroos explains:

> A number of M7s, or Priests, were acquired, the guns removed and additional armour welded into place.... Drivers for the converted [defrocked] Priests were gathered up from Artillery Units and Reinforcement groups, rushed to their vehicles, and despatched into action with no time for organizing or training.

The rush into action was such that on 28 August, 25 Kangaroos, 100 drivers, 4 officers, plus a Squadron Commander left for the Falaise Gap action in the Le Havre area with the British 51st Highland Division. The infantry suffered no casualties while they were inside the Kangaroos, thus giving the Kangaroos instant and widespread fame throughout the infantry.

Kangaroo

The Kangaroo was the brainchild of LGen Guy Simonds, commander 2nd Canadian Corps. De-turretted Priests or Ram tanks were used to carry infantrymen in these bullet and splinter-proof vehicles.

*From **Tools of War 1939/45***
1969 The Reader's Digest Association (Canada) Ltd. Montreal
Reproduced with permission

After that initial action near Rouen, France, a large number of Ram tanks were deturretted and converted to carriers. This vehicle was to become the most commonly used Kangaroo. After success at Boulogne and Calais, the 21st Army Group decided to increase the squadron to regimental size by 8 November 1944. The squadron now consisted of 53 Kangaroos, able to lift a full battalion of infantry. In December the unit "was transferred in to the 79th British Armoured Division, thus earning the distinction of being the only Canadian unit in this famous assault Division."

1st Canadian Armoured Personnel Carrier Regt. badge

When I looked at the Roll of Honour for this regiment, I was struck by the fact that only 13 men were killed between 17 September 1944 and 12 April 1945. Four died of wounds. The men of other battalions carried by Kangaroos onto objectives also suffered far less. The 1st Canadian Armoured Carrier Regiment was involved in 45 actions, and carried 38 different British battalions and 16 Canadian battalions "from Start Line to Objective at speed and with a minimum of casualties. The tactical handling of infantry in battle had been revolutionized by the Kangaroos!"

Arnold Bannister was released as a sergeant in August 1945. He has since died; his son John provided me with the details of this story.

The Sherbrooke Fusiliers on D-Day

On D-Day, 1944, "Bomber" Bateman was the Battle Captain of B Squadron, Sherbrooke Fusilier Regiment, 27th Canadian Armoured Regiment. The Sherbrookes went in on the second wave at about noon. In the tank named "Bomber", after the nickname of its crew commander, Bateman led his squadron. (All B Squadron tanks had names beginning with "B".) With the rest of the brigade, B Squadron was landed at Berniers and made its way south on the one road to Beny-sur-mer:

> We had had a very rough crossing; there was over a foot of water on the deck. When the ramp went down on the landing craft the tank had to move forward slowly and balance on the ramp, move ahead and then fall forward 11 feet into the water. [The tanks were water proofed and had intake and exhaust extensions that enabled them to travel through the water.]

Imagine the crew of five sealed inside their Sherman tank as it went through the water. The driver was in the left forward compartment, out of touch with the crew commander except for the intercom, which was part of the radio system. Then disaster struck:

> We had a self-netting device [to have all the radios on the same frequency] installed in all the troop leaders' tanks. All you had to do was press down a little switch and all the radios were fixed on net. When the signallers installed mine, a loose wire must have been left unattached and my radio shorted out and the turret filled with smoke. Here I was about to leave the landing craft and I could talk to no one, including the driver. I had to rig up two strings from the shoulder straps of my driver's uniform and pass them back through the turret to where I could steer my driver like a team of horses. It worked, we got ashore and I soon found a new radio.

Battle presented new problems. The tank crews had only cat naps for those first seven days, and they got those only if they were in a reserve position out of direct contact with the enemy. Bomber wore

Sherbrooke Fusilier Regiment

tightly laced rubber boots that caused his feet to swell like balloons, until walking was excruciatingly painful.

Bomber was impressed by the tight control held over the regiment by its commanding officer, LCol Mel Gordon, even during the strain of combat:

Mel Gordon felt very badly about our fatal losses but he didn't show any emotion. He personally wrote every letter to the next of kin; no one did it for him.

[Between 6 June and 8 July the regiment lost six officers and 35 other ranks.] He was hard on people who failed in battle. They just didn't stay in the regiment for a second. He worked on a regimental net. He could listen to everything first hand. He knew when a troop was engaging the enemy or a squadron needed assistance. His strength was the radio discipline he demanded from all of his tank crew commanders.

The action Bomber remembers best was when B Squadron led the night attack on Calcar. The official history says "The 6th Brigade's three battalions, all armour borne, crossed the start line, following a barrage which moved at tank pace.... Searchlights playing on the low clouds provided artificial moonlight." Bomber takes up the narrative, saying that the infantry, flame throwers and flails were all moving together and the flails came upon the gate at the entrance to Calcar!

There was water on both sides of the road. Barring our way was a huge stone wall, and the flails were too wide to go through it. Everything came to a halt. I rushed forward, ordering the flail troop leader to move out of the way. The

"Bomber" Bateman in Holland, 1945

enemy had withdrawn so we had to move on and seize the high ground. Much to the disgust of the British officer the flails moved into the water. We rushed on and seized the high ground just at first light. This whole exercise went as clockwork and our losses were very light. We repulsed the counterattack. As a squadron commander that action was my best battle.

Bomber Bateman remained in the Army after the war, going on to command the Royal Canadian Dragoons from 1975 to 1978, eventually becoming the Provost Marshal. After retiring from the Forces he commanded the Ottawa Corps of Commissionaires until June 1986. He is now retired and living in British Columbia.

The Dieppe Raid

More has been written about the Dieppe Raid than about any other battle in which Canadians fought and perished. The Allied situation in early 1942 was not good. The German advance into Russia was getting close to Leningrad; North Africa saw Rommel almost in Egypt; the much touted "Second Front" was still just words. It was decided at the highest level that a raid should be launched on Dieppe: "the raid would ... provide the opportunity to test new techniques and equipment, and be the means to gain experience and knowledge necessary for planning the great amphibious assault."

The raid was set for July 1942, but was cancelled due to bad weather, and many of the fully briefed troops were sent on leave. Hugh Comack of Winnipeg's Queen's Own Cameron Highlanders of Canada was one of those private soldiers:

We just got back from leave when we were ordered to go to Newhaven, Sussex, to put on a landing demonstration for some American troops. [This was a cover plan.] On the way, we were issued live ammunition -- we knew then that this wouldn't be any demonstration. The target was obvious, Dieppe.

When we got to Newhaven we boarded the "R" boats in an assembly area -- these boats were the six-ply boats equipped with two Ford V8 engines. You had to jump off over the front end onto the beach. I can remember going out to sea under the bridge at Newhaven about 8:45 p.m., and moving silently with the flotilla on the night crossing of the Channel. The invasion force crossed without incident -- it was one of the most beautiful mornings we had ever seen. About 4:00 a.m. we started to get ready. The Germans were getting ready too, and soon shells were coming at the flotilla. I remember Alex Graham, our piper and latterly the Pipe Major in the Cameron's Militia Band, playing the company march past -- "Hundred Pipers" -- as we approached the beach at Pourville. Alex was taken prisoner later that day. The first wave had already gone in -- our motors failed half a mile from the beach

63

and we had to be towed the rest of the way by a motor torpedo boat. I guess we were lucky, because we got right on to Green Beach, which was our target -- didn't even get our boots wet when we jumped down onto the shingle. Once on the beach we were soon pinned down by mortars and machine-guns from the east flank. On the way up to the beach wall I saw our Regimental Commanding Officer who had been killed by a burst of machine-gun fire. He led the way out of an assault boat and was cut down before he had taken more than a dozen steps.

The group Hugh was with tried to get through the barbed wire on the sea wall, but couldn't, so they decided to go down the beach and through a pillbox. Suddenly a large piece of shrapnel from a mortar bomb tore through the side of the wireless set Hugh was wearing on his back. The confusion worsened. Hugh couldn't locate B Company Headquarters, so he went with a C Company platoon. "It was then I remember seeing LCol Cecil Merritt on the bridge waving his hat." (Merritt was the CO of the South Saskatchewan Regiment.) Hugh realized later that he saw Merritt winning the VC for rallying his soldiers to continue the attack.

Confusion reigned. The Camerons were suffering many casualties, and the able-bodied started to evacuate them. The padre, Captain Jim Browne, worked as a stretcher bearer, trying to get the casualties to the beach. At 1100 hours the Camerons received an order to evacuate. The Canadians wanted to hold the perimeter, but the Germans had climbed to the heights and were firing down at them. It would have been suicide to remain. Hugh continues:

The last of the casualties I can remember carrying down to the beach was our Company Sergeant Major -- Nero Orlesky. We carried him and three other casualties down to the beach and dug them in for protection against mortar fire which was becoming quite heavy. The assault boats were starting to come back in. I remember Captain Jim Mulholland -- our Beachmaster -- who was doing a lot of directing while standing out on the open beach, trying to get the wounded off. I can also remember my Sergeant, Bill Rankin, though badly wounded, signalling the boats with a daylight signalling lamp. He never got off that beach -- he's buried in the cemetery at Rouen, having died of wounds shortly afterward.

Hugh's group saw three empty boats on the beach and ran out into the water to try to launch one. German fire pinned them down behind one. They started pulling it off the beach before they noticed there was a big hole in the bottom.

German fire was dangerously heavy down by the boats, so they decided to run back up the beach and get back under the wall. Hugh explained how they got away:

> Steeds -- was later killed in the Battle of the Hochwald -- was right beside me. He looked at me and said, "Let's go!" so we went hell bent for election for about 30 yards to the shelter of the sea wall. Finally two more boats came in and anchored about 50 yards down the shore. Steeds and I made a run for it across the beach for the third time. We swam out to an assault landing craft and, in getting over the ramp, the snipers got the chap next to me. As soon as we got into the boat, the mortars opened up, and they kept firing at us all the way back to the tank landing craft. In the boat somebody handed me a canteen and asked if I wanted a drink. I said I sure as hell did; it was pure Scotch.

German bombers kept after them all the way back to England. They had a great number of casualties on board, and two or three died on the way back. They arrived in Newhaven and docked about 2300 hours. When Hugh returned to the battalion the next day, he learned that of the 565 who embarked, only 98 or 99 had arrived back at camp in one piece. Others were casualties in hospital, dead, missing or taken prisoner. Hugh's final comment on the raid:

> I haven't any remorse about Dieppe. I believe now it was necessary. We tried out a lot of new equipment, new techniques. The lessons, though costly, were valuable to future operations. As far as I was concerned it was a job to be done. We knew it wasn't going to be easy and it wasn't. There is no room for remorse, that's not the true character of a soldier.

Hugh Comack left the Queen's Own Cameron Highlanders of Canada two years later to take his commission. He did not rejoin the unit during the war, but returned to it in Winnipeg in 1949. He was appointed Commanding Officer of the regiment in 1961, and in 1973 became Commander, Prairie Militia Area, as a Brigadier General. On 11 November 1977 he retired from the Army. Hugh lives in Winnipeg, Manitoba.

Germans inspect Canadian tank after Dieppe Raid

Send the POWs back to the FOO

Vic Thompson served in the 13th Field Artillery Regiment during the war. They had gone into action on D-Day and had supported the 3rd Division and the 7th Brigade for nearly six months when Vic nearly ended up in one of those neat and tidy war cemeteries.

It was on Friday, the 13th of October, 1944. Vic's story, taken from his Volume 3 of **Vignettes and Verse and Worse**, explains that he and his driver were off on an easy job to pick up a field gun when he was diverted to be a Forward Observation Officer [FOO] for the North Shore Regiment. When he found the North Shores, his Battery Commander said:

> "Well, your new job didn't last too long. It appears the North Shores consider you their good luck charm and they think they may need you for this seaborne assault. Hope you don't mind!" [Vic wrote], I am to travel as the FOO with C Company, and my carrier is backed onto a tracked amphibian -- the Alligator. We are soon floating in the tidal waters of the West Scheldt.

Things went well at the start, but then the Alligator got stuck on a sand bar. A German coastal gun at Walcheren decided to destroy Vic, his carrier and the Alligator. Fortunately, common sense prevailed on the Alligator. Realizing the danger of staying on their stranded vehicle, Vic and his cohorts waded to the shelter of the dyke. They had barely reached it when German shells set their vehicle ablaze. The day continued, and so does Vic's story:

> I attended the Company Commander's Orders at noon when he gave his orders for the attack. I am to arrange for the shells from my battery to fall on known and suspected strongpoints, beginning five minutes before H-Hour, which is at 1400 hours.

Vic had gone through the procedure so many times in training in England, and for real since 6 June 1944, that it had become second nature. The attack went in on foot with Vic walking some 300 yards behind the leading platoons. "The attack is going very well. POWs arrive, sent back by the platoons: 10, 20, 50, even more."

Something had to go wrong to ruin what had become a reasonable day in battle. It came from an unexpected quarter: "Out of the afternoon sky swooped the Typhoons [Allied close support fighters-bombers] aimed right at us." As Vic looked at the planes' 12 rockets heading straight for him, he thought, "No one can survive; this is it."

The rockets landed in and around the German POWs at Company Headquarters, but luckily the waterlogged earth absorbed most of the concussion and splinters. Vic continues, "I am the only Canadian casualty. One hot little needle [rocket splinter] in the hip, that's all. No pain, lots of sticky blood." The wound was dressed and Vic was taken back to the regimental doctor, who smiled and said, "You are my 2000th casualty since D-Day. You have a perfect Blighty [slang for Britain] wound, just enough to get you out of this hellhole."

Vic Thompson left the Army after the war, re-enlisted for Korea, and in 1957 became my CO when I worked with the Militia. After being retired for many years Vic died in Calgary, Alberta, in 1989.

25-pounder gun/howitzer

The 25-pounder was the workhorse of Commonwealth field artillery units. A six-man crew could get it into action in about one minute -- either as a gun, firing armour-piercing shells with a flat trajectory, or as a howitzer, firing high-explosive shells at a high angle. The gun was effective up to 12,500 yards; with a super-charger, up to 13,400.

From **Tools of War 1939/45**
1969 The Reader's Digest Association (Canada) Ltd. Montreal
Reproduced with permission

Smoke used to stop the fire

The duties of a Technical Staff Officer at an Army Corps Headquarters consisted of advising the staff on what could and what couldn't be done, and, if possible, how best to do it. That was the theory anyway, but military operations tend to make greater demands on soldiers than called for in job descriptions. This example from Northwest Europe in 1944 demonstrates that innovations and initiative beyond the letter of duty are required at the most unexpected times.

In September 1944, the 2nd Canadian Corps Technical Staff Officer, Jim Bond, was alerted to a problem foreseen by the senior artillery officer of the 3rd Canadian Infantry Division. BGen P.A.S. Todd was massing Allied artillery support for the assault on Calais. Unfortunately, the German gun positions at Cap Gris Nez, on the Canadian left flank, had been bypassed and were still operational. These positions contained coast defence and cross-channel guns of varying calibres. The problem given to Jim Bond was to screen the Allied gun area from this flanking fire. It was thought that a smoke screen might be required during daylight hours for one or two days. After a reconnaissance, Jim advised on the size of the smoke screen, where it should be located and what stores would be required.

At 1800 hours on 22 September Jim was told to implement his plan by first light the next day. For manpower, he was told that some gunners of a light anti-aircraft battery would be detailed to assist, and that some smoke pots would be provided. A Command Post was established and a detailed operational plan was made. During the night, the gunners arrived and some smoke pots were delivered.

By 0700 hours on 23 September the screen was in operation, and Jim spent as much time that day arranging for administrative support as he did on operational control of the screen. There was a minor crisis when one of the 14-inch German guns at Cap Gris Nez shelled Jim's Command Post area. A second crisis arose when Jim was informed that the screen would probably be required for five or six days. Fortunately, Jim remembered spotting German smoke pots in an ammunition dump

Jim Bond, November 1945

near Rouen. Arrangements were made to have these pots picked up and delivered overnight.

The smoke screen was maintained throughout 28 September with only minor problems due to wind shifts, a requirement to cut smoke during an RAF bombing of Cap Gris Nez on 26 and 27 September, and a continuing need to economize on the use of smoke pots caused by late deliveries of stores. In C.P. Stacey's **The Victory Campaign**, these lines attest to Jim Bond's actions: "A feature of the operation was the use of a smoke screen, 3000 yards long, to hide a number of artillery (Allied) units from observation from the German positions on Cap Gris Nez."

The smoke operation, which was deemed to have achieved its objective, was the first of many conducted by First Canadian Army. It was also one example of many proving that a Technical Staff Officer must go beyond his duties to lead, command and, not least, be innovative. Jim received a well deserved Mentioned in Despatches for his service during the operation.

Jim Bond remained in the Canadian Army after the war, retiring from the Armed Forces in 1968. At one stage of his career he served in Petawawa as my tank squadron commander with the Royal Canadian Dragoons. He is now a business consultant and lives in Ottawa.

Rockets at Flushing

When he served with the 6th Light Anti-Aircraft Regiment, RCA, Roy Bannister had the opportunity to use a unique new weapon. The story of the three-inch rocket began in the Navy, when it was used on landing craft to put down a massive fire pattern on the Normandy beaches. General Guy Simonds was impressed by what he saw and told his technical people in England to design a similar rocket system to be used on land. The design team took the wheels, frame and hitch of a water trailer, replaced the hitch with a split trail, and installed a levelling device and a rudimentary gun site. To this platform they welded brackets to hold rocket launcher tubes made from civilian oxygen bottles. As Roy described it, "The whole thing was Rube Goldberg at best." The rockets were to be fired not by cap and striker, but by electrical leads from the rear of the rocket. Pigtails were fastened to a firing sequence board made from a British telephone dialling mechanism hooked up to a battery. Thirty-two or 36 tubes contained the cordite-filled rockets. Screwed into the end of the rocket was a 3-inch artillery high-explosive shell. At the end of the shell was a fuse; the shell had "spoilers" or fins attached to give stability in flight. The rate of fire, once the firing sequence began, was one rocket every second; the entire weapon system cleared in less than 50 seconds.

Reloading was a long and laborious process. Roy explained, "We used mountains of ordnance, as there were two projectiles to a box, two rockets to a box, and other bits and pieces in another box. The convoy bringing up our ammunition took many trucks and they had to be deployed in the correct sequence behind the launcher. Everything had to be carried up by hand to the gun crew."

When the six projectors fired in the artillery battery, the high-pitched scream of the rockets was unbelievable. The three-inch shells landed in a very tight pattern, or mattress. (The unit was later designated the Canadian Land Mattress Battery, RCA.) The mattress had a devastating effect. "I never reloaded and fired again because there was no need." The damage caused by the dense concentration of explosives destroyed everything within the target area. Roy described a target sequence on Flushing:

The battery of six launchers pulled into a position behind a dike, and for that afternoon and all that night the crews loaded the launchers. By first light they were ready to fire the six launchers. The gunners could not see the Royal Marine assaulting troops. Once the assault force seized the objective, the battery moved on. One of the Royal Marine officers explained that the enemy coastal battery was in the process of a shift change when the mattress of shells landed. The enemy gun crews were all dead and a great many of them had no visible wounds; the blast had killed them outright.

Roy received word that his wife had died and he was to be allowed to return home. The red tape took so long that he was still in England when the war came to an end.

Roy Bannister remained in the Permanent Force and was on the staff of 66 LAA Regiment in Duncan, British Columbia, when I joined 198 Battery in 1947. Thirty years later we served together again when I was in a Militia support job in Ottawa. Roy died three years ago in British Columbia.

The three-inch rocket projector used by 6 LAA Regiment being readied by a crew such as the one commanded by Roy Bannister.
Photo courtesy CFB Shilo RCA Museum

Three VCs received her care

Nursing Sister Margaret Kellough of Toronto allowed me to tape-record an interview some years ago, but before this story could be written, her story was printed. Joyce Hibbert wrote about Margaret in **Fragments of War: Stories from Survivors of World War II**. Rather than repeat Hibbert's narrative, I have here recorded two anecdotes that were not printed.

In early 1942 while nursing at Bramshott, Hampshire, England, Captain Margaret Kellough had a padre for a patient. He had fallen from a motorcycle and had broken his right shoulder. With his arm in an airplane splint he would go down to the hospital victory vegetable garden and pump the stirrup pump, while a nurse, Marge Dewar, watered the rows of peas and carrots. That padre was John Foote of the Royal Hamilton Light Infantry. Some time later, during the Dieppe Raid on 19 August 1942, he was to save at least 30 lives. As the last boatload of survivors was leaving the beach to head for safety, John Foote jumped back in the water and splashed back to the men stranded on the beach, because, he said, "it seemed to me the men ashore would need me far more in captivity than any of those going home." For such outstanding courage, Padre Foote was awarded the Victoria Cross in 1945 when he was freed from captivity.

Margaret was the Assistant Matron when a Royal 22nd Regiment officer, Paul Triquet, was brought into 15 Canadian General Hospital (CGH) at Caserta, Italy. Margaret described the scene:

> With only field dressings on their wounds, some 200 men a day arrived straight from the battlefield. Some had been given morphine by their unit medical assistants, but most arrived just the way they had been hit. We were a 1200-bed hospital, but quite often we got as many as 1700 patients. The operating room staff worked eight hours on and eight off.

One day a group of Royal 22nd Regiment officers and other headquarters staff arrived at 15 CGH to see Paul Triquet. Margaret told them, "You will have to wait, as he has just gone to mass." Wait they did, and when he returned, they told him he had been awarded the Victoria Cross for his valour and battlefield leadership in early December 1944.

In January 1945, Capt Kellough was serving with No. 5 Canadian Casualty Clearing Station (CCS). The Nursing Services War Diary states: "Number of cases for the month, 206. The lads have been just as wonderful as ever. They certainly can take it." Margaret will never forget those men she cared for; they filled such a large portion of her young life. "Life was for earnest -- real hard work. There was no glamour in a CCS. You were just as likely to be shelled as not." One very wounded major who passed through 5 CCS was Fred Tilston, VC.

Margaret was awarded the Associate Royal Red Cross medal (ARRC), and some of the words in her citation were "An inspiration under most adverse conditions, ... her quiet efficiency and ready smile smoothing over many difficulties.... An example of self sacrifice and understanding, outstanding skill and leadership worthy of the highest praise."

John Foote in the airplane splint at Bramshott, 1942

Margaret Kellough when she joined the RCAMC

Margaret returned to Canada and left the Army in 1946. She worked as a nurse until she retired. She is still an active member of the Wartime Nurses Association, and can be found helping ex-nurses who are now patients in K2-E, the Veterans' Wing of Sunnybrook Hospital in Toronto.

Building bridges, clearing mines

Seven Platoon, C Company, Second Battalion, Royal Canadian Engineers, was the domain of Frank Barr for part of the Second World War. His unit landed at Courseulles and moved into the Caen area. Their first task was to make a road around Caen, because the bomb and shell damage was so great the rubble in the streets made road movement well nigh impossible. C Company built a "triple double Bailey bridge over the Orne River to link up with the ring road."

The next task for Frank's platoon was a vital one, requiring great skill and determination. The danger-filled job of clearing the mines and booby traps from Carpiquet airfield was up to them. As Reg Roy explained in his book **1944: The Canadians in Normandy**,

> The need for additional landing sites made Carpiquet airfield outside Caen a particularly valuable prize for the army commander. Since D-Day the entire area had been converted into a fortress zone by the Germans ... anti-aircraft posts, mines, machine-gun pill-boxes, and barbed wire.

The losses to the Canadians in clearing the airfield were considerable. Then the Engineers moved in.

Frank described the airfield as "a shambles; the hangars were twisted girders with German grenades, anti-personnel mines, unexploded bombs and even some unexploded 16-inch naval shells everywhere." This was the first time 7 Platoon had used dogs from the Royal Engineers' Dog Platoon. The dogs "had been trained to locate places where the mines had been placed. Each time they found one they were rewarded with a small piece of bully beef."

The mines that could not be lifted were detonated by flail tanks, huge drums fitted with long chains that flailed the ground in front of the tracks. The airfield was shelled by the Germans while the clearance project was underway, but finally "the job was done. We had removed 750 mines." The unit then started to repair the existing runways and build new ones.

Capt Frank Barr, England 1945.

Frank was to go on to other tasks of bridge building and route clearance. Then in Germany at Cleve he became involved in a critical operation. The Germans had so perfected booby traps on Tellermines that casualties in minefield clearing were high. Frank was sent in to determine how to pull the mines with safety:

I got lucky -- after pulling four mines with a 50-foot cable, the fifth one did not explode. After a few minutes I examined the mine hole; I noted a small circular metal disc (dime size) protruding one inch above the mine hole bottom. The 50-foot cable was attached with extreme care, then pulled, revealing a six-inch diameter metal canister. After whirling this against a pole (at the end of the 50-foot cable) with no explosion, I applied mine tools to the canister. The metal crimp had to be pried to open the canister. Suddenly -- a ticking sound! Faster work opened the canister, and I saw the striker hold wire being slowly withdrawn by a spring-loaded mechanism. This I bent 90 degrees and stopped the action. Thus, we had our first look at the "EZ44" anti-lifting device.

Frank's discovery changed the minefield gapping procedure; from then on they used flails, instead of engineers.

Frank Barr remained in the Army after the war. He retired as a Lieutenant Colonel in 1970 and then worked for the Public Service Commission. He is now retired and lives in Nepean, Ontario.

Prisoner for a day

An officer I greatly admired was a prisoner of war for less than a day. Bruce F. Macdonald commanded A squadron, The Fort Garry Horse. The Garrys had the distinction of "being the first Canadian Armour to fight in Germany".

In February 1945, A and B Squadrons were supporting the 4th Canadian Infantry Brigade in an attack on the Calcar -- Goch highway just south of Calcar, Germany. Things went badly for A Squadron on 19 February. During the morning, Macdonald's tank received a hit on the turret. He and his crew bailed out hastily, but as no flames appeared, they quickly returned to the safety of the tank. At 1300 hours the tank was hit again. Major Macdonald was wounded, and the badly damaged tank had to be abandoned. **Vanguard**, the wartime history of the Garrys, recorded the story:

> The Boches filtered into the attics of nearby buildings. There was little we could do but watch and wait. [Macdonald and his men were pinned down so could not withdraw and the crewmen were armed only with 9-mm pistols.] The Boche came, throwing grenades ... from 50 feet away and after most [of us] were wounded one stood up with his hands in the air and the rest of us followed suit.

Hurriedly, Macdonald stripped off his badges of rank, got rid of his binoculars, and tried "to look like a rather older trooper". His ruse paid off, for he was not separated from his men, was not properly searched and was marched off with the rest toward Appeldorn. While it was still dark, this tall, very conspicuous soldier "slipped into a convenient roadside ditch". As soon as the group had passed him by he retraced his steps back to where he had been captured and "arrived back in our lines in an exhausted condition" early in the morning.

Bruce Macdonald's powers of observation, sense of direction and almost photographic memory now held him in good stead. "He reported to the Corps Commander and told him what he had seen of the German defences and ground condition. It developed that [his] report on the 10 miles of countryside through which Second Canadian Corps was to advance that very day was of crucial importance in confirming the assault plan." It is no small wonder that Bruce Macdonald later received a well-earned DSO for his courage and devotion to duty.

Bruce F. Macdonald remained in the Army, becoming Director of Armour, Commander First Brigade, Commander of the Truce Commission in Pakistan, and retired as the Deputy Chief of Personnel in NDHQ. He died of Parkinson's disease in 1985.

Inside the Sherman

It was this type of tank used by the Fort Garry House, in the story of Bruce Macdonald. These cutaway illustrations show the positions of the crew of the Sherman medium tank (M4A2). The tank commander (A) is at the rear of the turret, just to the right of the 75-mm gun guard. Almost directly in front of him is the gunner (B). The loader (C) sits to the left of the 75-mm gun. In the left bow is the driver (D); the assistant driver (E) sits in the right bow, to the right of the transmission and behind the .30 bow machine-gun.

From **Tools of War 1939/45**
1969 The Reader's Digest Association (Canada) Ltd. Montreal
Reproduced with permission

Two padres, two battles

These stories of two padres, one in North West Europe, the other at Hong Kong, are dissimilar in content, but they reveal the same profound concern of the padres for their military parishes.

Joe Cardy was the padre with The Essex Scottish. The theme of his short narrative concerns his burial flag, a Union Jack he carried throughout his service with The Essex Scottish. He used the flag at each burial in the field of battle. It was even used as an altar cloth covering a manger in a small barn in France when he held a short church service just behind the front lines. The flag was given a front page story in the **Toronto Star**, 13 September 1944, when Frederick Griffin wrote about The Essex Scottish capturing Westende Plage, some six miles west of Ostend.

Union Jack

The German surrender was announced by the traditional white flags. Then the German soldiers marched raggedly out, weaponless and with hands high above their heads. That was when Padre Joe Cardy went into action with his battle flag. He "began clambering to the top of the command post to plant a Union Jack. He had the flag by chance with him at the moment, for he was about to hold the burial service for the one man killed when the surrender of the Germans took place."

Just as other officers were posted out of the regiment, so did their padre finally have to leave. Before going, he presented the regiment with his burial flag. It is now in the regimental chapel in the armouries in Windsor, Ontario.

While with The Essex Scottish, Padre Joe was awarded the Military Cross (MC) and was Mentioned in Despatches. Two paragraphs in the

MC citation show the measure of the man:

> In one particular attack, when casualties were heavy and all medical facilities were taxed to the utmost to care for wounded, Captain Cardy himself drove a 15 hundredweight truck out past our two foremost positions under heavy fire from enemy artillery, mortars and automatic weapons to bring casualties back for medical attention. Highly respected and admired by all ranks, he is an outstanding example of his own teaching that morale and character in the fighting soldier arise from a Way of Life. Insofar as the continued defeats inflicted on the enemy by The Essex Scottish Regiment have depended upon these factors, a large measure of success has been achieved through the unfailing and untiring devotion to duty of Honorary Captain Joseph Cardy.

Padre Joe Cardy remained in the Army after the war. He served as a major in Korea in 1952, and in 1968 he became the Chaplain General (Protestant) of the Canadian Forces. He retired in 1974 and now lives in Victoria, British Columbia.

The Hong Kong story is one of frustration, bravery and sorrow. **No Reason Why** by Carl Vincent examines the Hong Kong tragedy in detail, and I have used it as my primary source. Another reference is the personal diary of Padre Jim Barnett of the Royal Rifles of Canada. Padre Barnett's story begins 7 December 1941 in the peaceful colony of Hong Kong, and ends abruptly on 16 April 1942 with the entry: "Five months ago we arrived in Hong Kong, three weeks travel, three weeks free, three weeks fighting and then POW camp." Four years later, the appallingly few Canadians who were left returned home in ill health, many to remain in hospital until their death.

On 22 December the battle for the Island of Hong Kong began with heavy attacks by the Japanese. Jim was at St. Stephens Hospital: "Casualties pouring in. The news is not very good.... I find my work very interesting in the base hospital. Strange that I should serve in one at the end. I don't know whether I am doing right or wrong." That same day the padre worked in the operating room, and later buried a sergeant from the Winnipeg Grenadiers killed in battle.

On 23 December the Japanese net grew tighter as the Canadian troops pulled back. The many burials that day saw Jim helping dig the graves in Stanley Cemetery. The hospital was being shelled, so serious medical cases were moved to Stanley prison.

By the 24th, the Canadians were just about at the end of human limits. Vincent writes that men of the Royal Rifles of Canada "were collapsing with fatigue and exhaustion. The [unit had] done far more marching and fighting than any other component of the brigade." (This does not mean the Winnipeg Grenadiers did less; they were in the other Brigade.)

On Christmas Day the Japanese overran the hospital. Jim recorded: "They started to bayonet some patients in their beds." About 90 staff and wounded were "herded together in a very small room." The heat was unbearable, yet one man asked the padre to hold a Christmas service. "I told the Christmas story, said the Lord's Prayer [and the collect] for Christmas, and commended ourselves to God's keeping." The men shared a can of celery as their Christmas dinner.

Christmas Day brought surrender, and the men were allowed out of the small room. In the hospital, the padre built a funeral pyre and cremated his comrades who had been slaughtered by the Japanese. His last entry for the day: "I buried over a hundred bodies today."

So began the padre's life as a prisoner-of-war. His diary gradually grew shorter, the rumours more outlandish, hope dimmer. Carl Vincent summed up the Canadian action in Hong Kong this way:

> The two Canadian battalions performed the bulk of the fighting for the Island, particularly during the first five days.... The record speaks for itself. The Royal Rifles executed more counterattacks at company level or above then the British and Indian battalions combined, and the Winnipeg Grenadiers had the next greatest number. [If] the Canadians failed more, it was because they tried to do much more [than other units].

Just what was the price paid by the 1975 Canadians who left Vancouver to fight in the British colony? Five hundred fifty-seven did

81

not return. Over 100 died as prisoners in Hong Kong, and e˙en more died working in the mines of Japan.

I never met Padre Jim Barnett. I was planning a meeting with him in December 1984. He died while my wife and I were touring war cemeteries overseas. I will always regret that I did not manage to see him before he died.

All the way ... in one piece

Bill Elms of Toronto served in the 48th Highlanders as one of the Commanding Officer's drivers. Along with the First Canadian Division, Bill became part of the invasion force to cross the beaches of Sicily. Bill's story begins with the arrival of Regimental Transport in Sicily. LCol Ian Johnston had decided to travel in his Bren gun carrier, so Bill was left behind to move with the other wheeled (B) vehicles. The battle of Sicily ended when the Allies crossed the straits of Messina. Once again the CO left Bill behind, because small battle groups were more suited to the countryside and to the type of enemy action. [The CO decided to use the Bren-gun carrier sooner than his jeep.] Said Bill, "The B vehicles caught up to the rest of the battalion at Campobasso."

When I asked Bill to recall an event in which someone was very brave, but never rewarded for it, he said, "Soldiers who get on with the job even if it entails being extra brave never look around to see if someone is watching them." He did recall one night when "a sergeant went from slit trench to slit trench checking to see if his men were safe, and all the time we were being shelled." This brave man didn't need to expose himself to danger; no one would have remarked on it had he remained under cover. "That's leadership," summed up Bill.

Bill Elms, England; MGen Pearke's driver

By early 1943, after the battle for Ortona, the battalion was woefully understrength, down to 27 all ranks in a company. Bill explained, "People were just hanging on because they couldn't do anything else." Jaundice was rife, weakening everyone from divisional commanders to private soldiers. Somehow, Bill came through the war without a wound. "It was all around you, people falling, but not me." He agreed he had led a charmed life.

After the war Bill Elms returned to Toronto, but remained in the 48th Highlanders, becoming Drum Major, Regimental Sergeant Major and finally Regimental Sergeant Major of Central Militia Area. He retired from Ontario Hydro in 1986 and now works in the Regimental Museum of the 48th Highlanders.

Invasion of Kiska

Meeting of Generals by Tony Foster outlines the only invasion of the Second World War launched from Canadian soil. Brigadier Harry Foster came back from England to command 13 Canadian Infantry Brigade in a seaborne assault on the Japanese-held island of Kiska, a small dot at the end of the Aleutian Island chain. Tony Foster described the attack:

> By the spring of 1943 the Japanese garrison on Attu had 2500 men; Kiska slightly under 6000. The captured islands were like festering sores for the military psyche in Washington. Plans to retake them began. American troops landed on Attu on 11 May 1943 in one of the bloodiest assaults of the war up until that time.

The 24th Field Company Royal Canadian Engineers (RCE), commanded by Major Don Rochester, played a significant part in that assault. Don had been instructing RCE officers in Camp Petawawa before moving to Prince George, British Columbia. The RCE were then moved to Courtney, British Columbia, where they trained in amphibious operations. Don's company sailed with the invasion force on 10 July 1943 to Adak, an island about 200 miles east of Kiska. Various rehearsals were held, and then a preliminary bombardment by sea and air forces on 22 July and 2 August paved the way for an invasion on 15 and 16 August. According to **Six Years of War** by C.P. Stacey, the outcome of this invasion was a most welcome surprise:

> The landings took place as scheduled, but there was no opposition. The Japanese had decamped, and the invasion was a blow in the air. [Later intelligence revealed that] on 28 July ... the whole remaining force -- according to the best Japanese source, 5183 servicemen and civilians -- were jammed aboard the [2] cruisers and six destroyers [which took the Japanese] off in an hour.

BGen Harry Foster and LCol Scott Murdock climbed the heights above the beach after the unopposed landing. "They found the mountainside peppered with small caves. At the mouth of each, one or more machine-guns had been positioned.... Every well-oiled gun had an ammunition belt loaded and waiting to be fired." Scott Murdock said to the General, "Well, Boss, what do you think?" Foster's solemn reply summed up what could have been: "I think we're lucky to be alive."

Don Rochester's men had mixed emotions at finding the landing unopposed, but they had little time to think about it. Almost immediately they were handed a large task, to build a jetty so the island garrison could be resupplied. In Don's words:

Don Rochester - First Commanding Officer of The Canadian Airborne Regiment

The American Engineers and the United States Marines had started on a dock, but they pulled out. The Canadians were tasked to carry on and made such progress that the American docks were abandoned and the Canadian one was completed. It was 1700 feet long and 90 feet wide. It was pile driven and very well made.

The Canadians withdrew from Kiska and the Brigade was redeployed in Western Canada. Don Rochester went overseas to 8 Field Squadron in Germany and remained there until the end of the war.

Don remained in the Army serving in the Northwest Highways System, Korea and the Middle East. He was the first CO of the Canadian Airborne Regiment. Today, he is retired and lives in Vedder Crossing, British Columbia.

A General remembers

In 1984 I conducted a series of interviews with Lieutenant General E.L.M. Burns of Manotick, Ontario. General Burns served as a front line communications officer in the First World War, as a regular officer between the two World Wars, and as a brigade, divisional and corps commander in the Second World War. After the war he had a distinguished career as a United Nations soldier, a public servant and a peacemaker of world acclaim. What follows are some salient ideas from this great gentleman.

In speaking about the popularity of a general, Burns contended that "confidence in, sooner than popularity, was the key to the relationship between the led and their leader. Success in operations is what produces confidence. Success must be won on the field of battle and not fabricated by public relations organizations."

J.L. Ralston, the Minister of Defence, visited Italy in 1944 to see for himself just how badly reinforcement shortages were harming the front line combat units. On 30 September 1944, Ralston was told that "by 10 October there would be no infantry reinforcements left". How did this crisis affect the units of First Canadian Corps? General Burns:

> My infantry commanders were against going to a three-company battalion organization like the British had been forced to adopt. I expect that all my infantry officers felt this way, as they were the first to feel the lack of reinforcements. Once a battalion has to reduce its firepower because of understrength platoons and companies, it puts the entire manoeuvre and firepower system out of balance. Casualties increase, because the fire and movement so essential to the infantry just is not efficient.

The shortage of infantry soldiers and the uncertainty of reinforcements after D-Day in Europe caused General Burns serious problems. In the last year of the First World War, Burns had seen the Canadian Army bleed itself white because of the shortage of reinforcements, and it was painfully obvious to him that the same thing was happening 26 years later. Without weakening battle formations, he nonetheless had to try to preserve what men he had left. The General once remarked that "to send men to their certain death because of shortages of supporting artillery, ammunition and tank support, plus weakened understrength infantry battalions, was not good generalship and should be resisted."

In October 1944 General Burns was relieved of command of the Canadian Corps by Britain's General McCreery.

McCreery wanted to win, regardless of cost, and he didn't believe that General Burns had "the determination to drive the Canadian Corps ahead with the similar ruthlessness" McCreery had shown when he commanded 10 British Corps. With Burns trying to preserve men and McCreery wanting to put all available forces into battle, the two were at odds. As the Canadian in a British Army area, Burns lost out. Looking back to October 1944, Burns blamed no one for what happened. He said, "I lacked experience commanding a brigade and division in battle. It is not surprising they [the British] had their doubts. There is no doubt that the British felt if they had had the Canadian troops to handle they would have had greater success and personal credit." The British never wanted a Canadian Corps Headquarters in Italy in the first place, and its very existence stopped them from using Canadian formations with a free hand.

As his final comment on the event, the General repeated an observation he had written years before in **General Mud**:

> At the time I was very resentful of the way in which my service in the Italian Theatre had been terminated. Now I can look at it in a more philosophical way. It had the result, after the war was over, of setting my life on another course, which permitted me to serve the country in ways in which I may have been more useful than I could have been if I had gone on until the end of the war as Commander of the 1st Canadian Corps.

General Burns went on to fulfil that prophecy he made on leaving Italy in 1944. As Deputy Minister of Veterans Affairs, he fought and won many battles for Canadian veterans. I was fortunate to serve in the United Nations Emergency Force and established by General Burns. We were a force of many nations dedicated to a common goal, to maintain the peace between Arab and Israeli. General Burns was world renowned as a peacekeeper in the Middle East. In 1960 he became Canada's advisor on disarmament in Geneva. His five books are all classics in their field.

When General Tommy Burns died, tributes poured in from across Canada and around the world. J. King Gordon wrote in **A Soldier for Peace**, "I never found him dour. Quiet, yes. Serious, yes. No small talk. But not a difficult man to talk with. A clear concise mind." For my own part, I must add that General Burns "looked back" for me, and thus helped to form a big part of the stories I have passed on in the pages of this book.

Colonel Gardam interviews LGen E.L.M. Burns 19 December 1984

Fifty Years After

LGeneral E.L.M. Burns died at the age of 88 on 13 September 1985. At his funeral in Manotick, soldiers, statesmen, members of the United Nations and a Canadian Engineer honour guard saw a great Canadian go to his just reward.

Chapter Four

The Royal Canadian Air Force
(Eight members of the Light Blue)

The Royal Canadian Air Force was the smallest of the three services in 1939. More Canadians were flying with the Royal Air Force than with the RCAF, an unusual situation which was to continue throughout the war. In 1940 Canadian Fighter and Army Co-operation squadrons were in Britain when the Battle of Britain started and the Luftwaffe began trying to bomb Britain into submission.

In Canada, the British Commonwealth Air Training Plan (BCATP) was agreed to just three months after the war began. The BCATP was a great success, as aircrew could be trained well away from the air battles over Europe. Canada became one huge airfield. RCAF and civilian instructors produced almost 137,000 trained aircrew by the end of the war, 55 percent from Canada, the rest from all over the Commonwealth and even Norway.

As the war entered its early stages, three Canadian squadrons were sent overseas. This number increased to 48 with RCAF squadrons serving in the Mediterranean, the Far East and Europe. Coastal Patrol, Bomber Command and Fighter Command were the main areas of deployment, but the enormous training commitment also employed many Canadians. The biggest and costliest, in human losses, was Bomber Command. From 5 March to 24 June 1943, Number 6 Bomber Group lost 100 aircraft. Almost 10,000 Canadians lost their lives while flying in bombers.

The RCAF overseas came under the operational control of the RAF, but thousands of RCAF aircrew flew with RAF, RAAF and RNZAF Squadrons. There are RCAF buried in 74 countries of the world, a solemn testimony to their scope of involvement.

Fifty Years After

The stories in this chapter deal with many of the jobs and theatres not covered in official histories. They span pre-war to post-war, yet are but a minute sample of the RCAF at war.

Pre-war to post-war

When the Second World War broke out in the autumn of 1939, Schuyler "Sky" Thompson already had two years of service in the RCAF. He was serving in Ottawa as clerk to the RCAF Aircraft Inspector at the Ottawa Car and Aircraft Factory, where 18 Wapiti and a number of Avro 626s and 621s were being overhauled. When the overhauls were completed, the aero engines were "run up" on a test bed. The noise travelled from the RCAF Repair Depot on Victoria Island to Parliament Hill, much to the consternation of the sitting members. Upon completion of overhaul, the planes were towed to RCAF Station Rockcliffe, where they were flight tested for airworthiness. Sky mentioned that before one flight test he signed the necessary form absolving the Crown from responsibility in case of accident and was thereby permitted to go aloft as a passenger in a Wapiti.

> The pilot took me up approximately 8000 feet and headed out over the Gatineau Hills. We flew on and on and I thought what a fine fellow this pilot was giving me such a nice long flip, when the previous ones had been all too short, to my way of thinking. In the cockpit, I noticed that the pilot was working furiously at something or other, and I thought how conscientiously he was applying himself to his flying duties. At long last we turned back and made a nice three-point landing. Once upon the ground I went up to the pilot to thank him for the excellent trip. He simply took off his helmet, mopped his brow with his handkerchief, and said, "Young fellow, don't stand there and thank me! You should be thanking the good Lord that you are still in the land of the living. Do you know what happened up yonder? Well, the controls jammed, and if we had not been flying on a straight level course instead of up or down, your remains would now be being picked over with relish by some stray wolves in those hills." This should have deterred me from seeking further flights -- but it never did.

The Wapiti dropping bombs

RCAF HQ in Ottawa was hectic in those early months of the war, for they were organizing an overseas Headquarters to be established in Canada House, London, England. In February 1940, Cpl Thompson was ordered to report to the Commanding Officer, RCAF Repair Depot, Ottawa, where he was informed that he was to be posted overseas, "destination secret". Sky was elated. After a short embarkation leave of five whole days, he reported to Lansdowne Park, Ottawa, where he was told he had been promoted to sergeant. He and the other chosen few were confined to the Pure Food Building, so they could not inform anyone they were on draft for overseas.

> The day we left, prior to departure for the railway station, we attended a church service on the exhibition site and lustily sang the hymn which contained the words "for those in peril on the sea" -- very appropriate for what lay ahead. Before departing the park we were in one of the buildings polishing up on our drill under the supervision of a very competent drill instructor, when, unannounced, the RCAF Inspector General, AVM Croil, appeared in the doorway. The instructor's mind went blank and he marched us right into the wall! Later, upon reaching Union Station, we were

overwhelmed by the sight of our railway coaches -- they were the wooden seated type that the early immigrants were allotted in settler days. Despite the secrecy of our departure, a goodly number of people were on hand to wave goodbye. Among them were quite a number of girlfriends.

The train reached St John, New Brunswick, on an exceptionally cold night, and the draft embarked on the *Duchess of Richmond* for what proved to be a very rough crossing to Liverpool. Once in London, the Headquarters staff moved into Canada House, Sun Life Building, Trafalgar Square, under the command of Air Commodore G.V. Walsh.

"Sky" Thompson, England, 1941

Sky's memories of service in London during the blitz are rich in exciting and terrifying recollections. He saw a German plane bomb Buckingham Palace, searched for unexploded bombs in the backyard of his lodgings and got to know the Canadian High Commissioner and Mrs Vincent Massey quite well.

One duty performed by non-commissioned members was aircraft lookout warden on the roof of Canada House. Sgt Thompson was on duty the day the Palace was bombed and he pressed all the warning buttons to send the staffs of Air Force HQ, Naval HQ and Army HQ and the Canadian High Commissioners' staff racing to the basement air-raid shelter. He remembers, "If it had not been for the fear of the event, I would have taken a certain amount of pride in getting all that senior brass to move on the double."

As the Battle of Britain progressed, officer pilots started arriving in England from Canada. Sky was in charge of officer records, and he remembers taking down the particulars of the various individuals, such as next-of-kin. Just weeks later he was helping the padre inform the families of those same young men that they had been killed, were missing, or had been taken prisoner. A former roommate of his from Ottawa arrived with his wings up and claiming "that the war was as good as won now that he had arrived". Unfortunately he was shot down on his very first mission and spent the rest of the war as a prisoner of the Germans.

Additional personnel arrived in London from Canada as the Headquarters expanded. WO1 Thompson was posted back to Canada to serve in Montreal and Toronto. Sky was College Warrant Officer at RCAF Staff College, Toronto, during its early organization and was stationed there when the war ended.

Sky Thompson first took the Oath of Allegiance in the Frontenac Regiment, Napanee, Ontario in April 1929. Without a break, he went on to serve with the Haliburton Regiment and the Hastings and Prince Edward Regiment. He joined the (Permanent) RCAF in April, 1937 and retired from the Forces in 1969. While on retirement leave he joined the Public Service. He retired again in 1979, after 50 years of service to the Crown, and now resides in Ottawa.

Flying over North Africa

Lorne Haunts wanted to join the RCAF as a mechanic, but the recruiting officer in Kingston, Ontario, convinced him to try for aircrew. On 3 October 1940 he was posted to Brandon for aircrew ground training, but an ear infection often kept him out of the classroom. Regardless of Lorne's medical situation and inadequate training, the rapidly expanding British Commonwealth Air Training Plan resulted in a hasty move for Lorne on 14 October to Initial Training School for six weeks' training. Then he went on to Primary Flying School at Lethbridge. In just days Lorne had his first flight in a Tiger Moth. The civilian instructors were paid for each student, so they pushed their students through quickly.

In what seemed like no time, Lorne was told to take up a Moth for his first solo flight:

> I was at the end of the runway, just ready to take off, and I got a red light. Flying was washed out, which was a good thing in my case, as I would have killed myself. I was not ready to fly. On 12 December I was "ceased training" due to lack of depth perception. The chief superintendent said if they took more time I might make it, but I would never be a great pilot. I now faced a change in aircrew training. On 6th June 1941 I left for Regina and radio training, then went on to Rivers, Manitoba, to Navigation School. This is where I received the coveted 0 Wing as a sergeant. My total flying time by then was 119 hours.

> On 6 August 1941 I was posted to Halifax and on the 20th we boarded the armed merchantman *Worcestershire* and sailed with a three-knot convoy [50 ships]. The *Worcestershire* left the convoy and went to Iceland. We left that ship and went aboard the *Leopoldville* and sailed for England. We guarded the crew of a German U-Boat that had been forced to surface and surrender near Iceland. Scotland was the place of entry, and then on to Bournemouth.

When Lorne's first anniversary in the RCAF came he was already with an operational training flight near Stratford flying in Wellingtons. The airfield was on an English farmyard, with the owner and his family still in residence. Naturally enough, with all the young men about, the farmer worried about someone taking off with his daughters. "We left the girls alone," said Lorne, "but stole his chickens and got the farmer's wife to cook them for a special meal for us."

A few months later Lorne was posted to Cairo. His flight to Cairo began on 1 April 1942. Over the Bay of Biscay, Lorne realised that the pilot, who didn't trust Canadians, was not following Lorne's course. Finally, after 12 hours, 19 minutes of flying, when they were somewhere over Morocco, the pilot panicked. With their time of arrival for Malta already long overdue, the pilot turned back to Gibraltar. They landed with just five minutes' gas left.

Infuriated by their narrow escape, the crew wanted to split up and find their own ways to Cairo, abandoning the pilot, but the luxury of choice wasn't theirs. The next morning they took off together for Malta. This time the pilot followed Lorne's course, and the aircraft arrived at Malta right on time -- in the midst of an air raid. Another crew took their plane, and they were stranded in Malta till another Wellington landed. They finally made it to the landing field outside Cairo on 6 April 1942.

After a brief stint at a training area becoming familiar with desert flying, Lorne's crew was posted to 40 Squadron, RAF. Their first operational flight was a few days later; the target, Sidi Barani.

When Tobruk fell to the Germans it became one of the major targets of 40 Squadron. One special mission against the docks at Tobruk Harbour took place on 18 September 1942. As navigator, Lorne brought the plane on track through the south of the harbour, then, doubling as bombaimer, he made sure the bombs fell on their target, the fuel storage area. Aerial photographs attested to the accuracy of Lorne's bombs: severe damage indicated that the enemy's much-needed fuel had gone up in flames.

Lorne Haunts was awarded the Distinguished Flying Medal for the repeated excellence of his performance. The **London Gazette** quoted the citation, given here in part:

The work of this navigator has been outstanding. He has always performed his duties with quiet daring and courage. In many attacks over Tobruk against the harbour and shipping he was credited with firing a petrol dump.

Night after night, 40 Squadron bombed targets in the battle area. In April 1942 alone, over 50 hours of night flying completed nine missions. An exciting mission on the 29th was described curtly in the log: "Landed at 224 to pick up X." Those few words indicated a landing at an emergency strip behind enemy lines to pick up a secret agent. By 10 November 1942, 35 operational missions -- 230 flying hours -- had been flown.

The time-expired crew was sent back to England in November. Lorne learned of his commission when he saw it in the **London Times**.

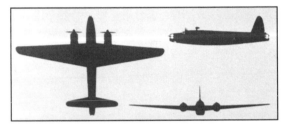

Picking up the **Gazette**, he then discovered the citation for his DFM. A short while later, Lorne answered the call for navigators to return to Canada to become

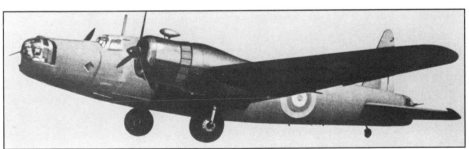

Vickers Wellington

Before the four-engine heavies took over, the faithful Wimpey was the backbone of Bomber Command and saw service with several Canadian squadrons. First flown in 1936, it had a rugged geodetic (lattice-work) frame which could withstand heavy punishment from enemy flak. It flew on its first bombing raid on 4 September 1939 and was still going strong as a front line bomber in Italy in March 1945.

From **Tools of War 1939/45**
1969 The Reader's Digest Association (Canada) Ltd. Montreal
Reproduced with permission

99

Lorne Haunts about the time he was awarded the DFM

instructors. After sailing home on the *Empress of Scotland*, Lorne served as an instructor at Rivers, Manitoba, and Rockcliffe, Ontario. He was discharged at the end of the war.

Lorne Haunts married Ruth Beswich, a corporal at RCAF Station Rockcliffe, and they have lived in Kingston, Ontario, ever since. Lorne remained with the Air Cadets from 1949 to 1969, finally hanging up his uniform after 26 years of service.

Radar in the Far East

During the Second World War, Canada had no radar stations of its own. The RAF used Commonwealth airmen to man radar stations throughout the world. This story concerns radar in the Far East.

It is a long way from Ottawa, Ontario, to Chittagong in India, but that was the wartime path taken by a young Canadian. Gordon Bourne of Ottawa tried to enlist in the Navy and the Army before finally being accepted by the RCAF. His particular skills as an amateur radio operator resulted in his being selected for Radio Direction Finding training in the Air Force. The entire trade was so secret that until Gordon reached England, he received almost no training in radar. In England, Gordon did well on his course, and was posted to the Far East as a radar mechanic with the RAF.

In January 1943 Gordon found himself en route to Calcutta to assemble a mobile radar in a camp by the sea, where he found the crabs poisonous, the water infested with sharks and a leopard roaming the camp at night. No sign of the Japanese Army, but the local wildlife sure was a challenge! Job completed, he was sent to a new site and another radar, but this time the enemy was at hand. Japanese snipers caused a fire fight, which resulted in the radar unit being in no man's land:

> Our radar was guarded by infantry and artillery units with 40-mm Bofors guns. This night an infantry patrol returned to explain they had heard something moving in the jungle, so the artillery unit opened fire along the nearby road. There was a Lancer [tank] unit at the other end of the road. The two units fired at each other over the heads of the airmen at the radar site. The radar Commanding Officer [CO] crawled to one unit and explained that "friends" were shooting at each other and he got the battle stopped.

Gordon's stories of the Far East are colourful. A corporal in Gordon's radar unit, John Russell, was a concert pianist. On one occasion he was ordered to perform at a concert for all the local officers and the Viceroy of India. When the Viceroy mentioned how

101

well the corporal played, the RAF CO said, "Yes, he does play well, considering he's only a corporal!"

Another of Gordon's friends had a Master's degree in Fine Arts, but deliberately failed his commission entrance examinations because he wanted to remain "one of the men". When he was promoted to AC1 he was livid, but that promotion was automatic.

Sgt. Gordon Bourne, India 1944

The radar Gordon tested and calibrated daily was the key to the RAF's defence of the Far East. Radar operators had to be able to scan Akyab Island 300 miles away. When the Japanese planes started to come over British-held territory in waves of 12 and 24 the radar operators were able to give advance warning to British anti-aircraft artillery. One First World War RAF pilot who wanted some excitement took up a Lysander -- top speed 260 mph -- and flew over a Japanese base, throwing small bombs out of the cockpit. He flew back without having drawn a single shot from the enemy. No doubt the Japanese were laughing too hard to react.

Gordon's total combat time was about 45 minutes, and much of that was during one Japanese air raid when his radar site was bombed.

Sickness took its toll, and Gordon was one of many invalided out of India, spending Christmas 1944 in Bombay and then travelling back to England via the Suez Canal. He returned to Canada by way of New York City and was eventually discharged in August 1945.

Gordon Bourne is retired and lives in Belleville, Ontario. In one of many federal government jobs he was responsible for quality control of electronic components for various radar stations across Canada. The training he had received in England helped him deal with the various electronics companies building and installing radar systems.

Spitfire

Bob Lacerte joined the RCAF in Saskatoon but took his primary flying training in Regina. Though they graduated with 33 others, Bob and a friend did not go on to Yorkton for bomber training. They had buzzed a train as it crossed Saskatchewan, and an air force officer had copied down their plane numbers and reported them. The result was that Bob and his friend went to St Hubert, Quebec, where they trained as fighter pilots in Harvards.

Bob recalled one mission in particular from his St Hubert days:

My instructor and I were flying the triangle -- Montreal, Ottawa, Cornwall, Montreal -- at night. We picked up a strong tail wind out of Ottawa and the next thing we were in dense cloud. We came down to try to pick up our location and we hit a mountain top in northern New York State. We were way south of where we were supposed to be. The instructor was badly hurt, but I managed to get him out of the plane, get a fire going and render first aid. Rescue found us and the instructor lived!

For saving the other man's life despite the pain of his own injuries, Bob received a King's Commendation.

When Bob was fit enough to graduate, he moved up to training on Hurricane fighters. Then he was posted to his first operational unit, 130 Fighter Squadron at RCAF Station Bagotville, Quebec. "We had two missions," said Bob, "fly air cover over the aluminum plant at Arvida and watch for German submarines in the St Lawrence River." They did sight one submarine, but caused it no damage.

In the spring of 1943, Bob was posted to England, where he converted to the Mark V Spitfire. His first overseas operational task was to become familiar with the Army, for he was to fly Army Co-operation and close support. Sessions with Army units, and escape and evasion courses followed, and then in June 1944 he was posted as a reinforcement pilot to 441 Squadron in France. Their aircraft were the Mark IX Spitfires fitted with bomb racks and a 20-mm cannon.

On 27 July Bob had his first shared kill, a Focke Wulf 190 just west of Caen. His log book for a week later, 4 August 1944, records four sorties when the Allies tried to close the Falaise Gap. The Allied advance out of Normandy meant 441 Squadron moved from airfield to airfield. By mid-September, Bob's squadron was flying fighter cover over the Arnhem airborne landing area.

Bob Lacerte

As he flew near the front line, Bob could see the soldiers below him: "When I saw what the soldiers were going through as their perimeter got smaller and tighter I was glad I was up where I was and not down there. The flak was so heavy that we were kept much higher than usual."

On 2 November 1944 Bob flew his final operational mission. His "weapon" was a cine gun, and he filmed a close air support mission. Just a few days after that mission Bob came down with pneumonia and had to be taken off flying. He left England late in November for Canada and the Colonel Belcher Hospital in Calgary. He remained in hospital for a year and a half with tuberculosis.

The war was over before Bob left the RCAF. He became a teacher and staunch supporter of the Chilliwack Air Cadet Squadron. He is now retired and lives in Chilliwack, British Columbia.

Guard duty at -40 degrees

When Frank Willard joined the RCAF in June 1940, he soon learned that to have put "shop keeper" as his civilian trade was to relegate himself to "Canada only" service and a career in stores.

Like so many servicemen from Ontario, Frank found himself doing guard duty at the Canadian National Exhibition grounds in Toronto. In those early days the RCAF issued Ross Rifles (the Lee-Enfields having been withdrawn after Dunkirk). To save the young men from shooting off rounds inadvertently, a wooden plug had been inserted in the breech. Nonetheless, the men were required to carry three rounds in their greatcoat pockets.

Later on, security officers had us equipped with the rifle and bayonet, but minus ammo. We were instructed to yell out our post number followed by "All's Well" at half-hour intervals. Shades of the Middle Ages! We were first posted around the officers' quarters and after three nights of hollering we were withdrawn, sleep being more important to them than their security.

St Thomas, Ontario, was where Frank took his Trades training. On graduation he requested "overseas or Winnipeg". Winnipeg it was to be: 7 Equipment Repair Depot. On Arrival at Number 7 Frank was again assigned to guard duty.

The depot was enclosed by a high wire-mesh fence. The perimeter around the depot was just over a mile. The west and south sides faced out on open prairie; the north faced on Notre Dame Avenue, a very busy artery: and the east side on to a dark, little-used lane. Lights were placed some 40 feet back from the fence outside. Along the fence at intervals were placed more powerful lights on 20-foot poles, shining down and inward. In between the sheds and fence with all the lights focused on them were sentries who could not see outside the fence because of the lights. Boy, were we sitting ducks for anyone wishing to do harm to the Depot and yours truly!

Frank drew the cartoon shown with this story. His recollection of those cold nights was "When it hit minus 40 degrees Fahrenheit in January, you rested your rifle against the sentry box and hugged the oil drum full of red hot coal. After 11:30 p.m. the Officer of the Day had made his final rounds and you were home free until 6 a.m."

Frank remained in Winnipeg for over two years before being sent to RCAF Station Trenton, Ontario, until the war ended. In Trenton, Frank had the unenviable job of Barrack Stores NCO, responsible for control of all stores. The job was made more difficult by the airmen trying to take extra supplies when they left for overseas. But, said Frank, "I never lost even one blanket in all the time I was there."

Frank remembers his relief on VE-Day and again on VJ-Day. He saw the rush and confusion as airmen lined up for release. But Frank's job was critical to orderly disbandment, so he remained. Married and with a family, 39-year-old Frank was anxious to return home. A kindly WO1 took pity and arranged Frank's release. With a railway travel warrant to Dryden, Ontario, in his hand, Sgt Frank Willard left the RCAF and returned home.

Frank Willard became a lab technician at the pulp and paper mill in Dryden. His art was an important part of his life, and his work can be seen in and around the Dryden area. Frank died in 1989.

The Happy Warrior

The sole survivor

Gordon MacDonald joined the RCAF in December 1941 after his first year at Victoria College in Victoria, British Columbia. His training took him to Number 3 Manning Depot in Edmonton and then on to Stanley, Nova Scotia, for pilot training. He was washed out as a pilot for unauthorized low flying, but remustered as a navigator. That training was conducted at Crumlin near London, Ontario. After graduation in December 1942, Gordon was posted overseas to England. He converted to the Stirling bomber and was posted to 75 Royal New Zealand Bomber Squadron near St. Ives in the Midlands. His first mission as WO2 MacDonald was a mine-laying operation in June 1943. The crew were RAF except for Gordon and the bombaimer who were RCAF -- none was a New Zealander.

The crew quickly completed 12 missions, mine-laying and bombing Brest, doodlebug sites and cities in the heart of Germany. Gordon was offered a commission, but he turned it down because he "would have been the only officer in the crew".

After conversion to the Lancaster bomber, Gordon was posted to 514 Bomber Squadron, RAF, at Cambridge. The raids went much deeper into Germany, far more planes were being used, and the flights were usually at night. WO1 MacDonald's seventh mission with 514 Squadron was to be his last and final event of the war:

The last mission for me was against Nuremburg, Germany, on 30/31 March 1944. We had been briefed for the raid two days in a row but it had been cancelled. We were told that it was suspected that German fifth columnists knew of the target and had forewarned the enemy that we were coming. We had our 1000 hours briefing and took off just after dark. The plane was flying beautifully, but there was a moon and we did not like flying under a full moon. We were over the Ruhr en route to our turning point 100 miles north of Nuremburg when we noticed there were a lot of German fighters aloft. I saw other aircraft being shot down and I timed the time from being hit to the explosion when the bomber hit the ground. I was also looking for parachutes to see if any of the crews had got out. It was taking 60 seconds from hit to crash! We were at 20,000 feet and we could see aircraft everywhere. We passed the turning point, a green flare dropped by the Pathfinders. We just knew something had gone wrong; the Germans were waiting for us! The rear gunner called "Starboard go", the pilot threw the plane sideways into a corkscrew, and I fell against the navigation table, but I saw a Junkers 88 coming for us. The wireless operator called out, "There is another fighter coming toward us." We were on our second corkscrew when the second fighter fired and hit our starboard engines, which caught on fire. The engineer hit the fire extinguisher switches which seemed to help for a moment. Then both JU 88s hit us again, the entire length of the aircraft this time, and the fire flared up again and we were engulfed in flames. The pilot called out, "Prepare to abandon." I got the pilot's chute onto him, but then the starboard wing collapsed and we went upside down. I knew we had 60 seconds before crashing. It was terrifying! Everything I did at that moment was automatic, just the way we had trained. I used my boots to break the roof cupola, as I knew I had to go out feet first. The G forces were so strong that I had to use strength I did not know I had. I can't remember leaving the aircraft for I had hit my head on something. I woke up on the ground with the parachute D ring in my hand, the parachute in tatters; I don't know how it held me up. I couldn't hear anything. I packed the chute into a hay stack to hide it. I was crawling, bleeding from the head, had no shoes and my head ached. I saw a woman screaming at me but I could not hear her. [Gordon did not gain back his hearing for three months.] I moved as fast as I could from furrow to furrow. I reached a stream and walked in it for an hour to hide my tracks. I saw no sign of my fellow crew members.

In his book **A Thousand Shall Fall**, Murray Peden wrote:

On the night of March 30-31, a night of bright moonlight and extremely high winds that scattered Main Force, Bomber Command attacked Nuremburg, despatching a force of almost 800 aircraft. Ninety-four failed to return, most of them the prey of the murderously efficient German night fighters. Ninety-four crews; 94 four-engined bombers. It was Bomber Command's worst loss of the war.

Gordon used every lesson he had been taught on escape and evasion exercises in England to elude the Germans. On his seventh day, after walking some 100 miles, Gordon was found asleep covered with leaves in a wood by German children playing cowboys and Indians. Their father used a pitchfork to prod him to the police. Gordon was moved from camp to camp until he ended up at Stalag 357 at Fallinbostel. **The POW Journal,** Winter 1986/87, gives this account:

By mid 1944 the Germans were being squeezed on all fronts... causing mass evacuations of POW camps. By February 1945 camps were in a deplorable state. By April 19th the British Second Army was on the line of the River Weser. With little warning, the POWs were marched out of the camp and away toward the Elbe.

WOII Gordon MacDonald awaiting transport to England after being found by advancing British troops on 5 May 1945. He is wearing a hat he made himself.

Gordon was one of those marching when, suddenly, on 5 May, "the guards disappeared". A group of the POWs stole a fire engine, marked it EX POW on one side and started to drive to meet the British Second Army. "They met us," said Gordon, "with white bread, jam and tea." It was a fast move back to England, and during a medical examination they were asked if "they had any medical problems which would prevent them leaving for Canada the next day." No one had any problems! In England, Gordon learned he had been commissioned while in POW camp. He also found out he was the sole survivor of his crew. Gordon was back in Halifax by mid-June 1945, having volunteered to go to fight Japan.

Gordon MacDonald transferred to the Canadian Army, joining the Royal Canadian Ordnance Corps. He served in Korea and Japan in 1953. Gordon retired from the Forces in 1972 as a major at CFB Rockcliffe. He is now retired and lives in Nepean, Ontario.

Flying with the Moosemen

During the summer of 1984 I met Merv Fleming researching the wartime casualties of 419 Moose Squadron. I asked him for his recollections of the life of a wartime squadron commander. I have condensed his graphic account:

> The Hollywood depiction of bomber operations leaves one with the impression that actual raids on enemy territory were the only occupation of operational air crews and their leaders. While such activities were the focus of all others, the days and nights of these men were filled with a variety of duties depending upon whether one was a gunner, a radio operator, a bombaimer, a navigator or a pilot and whether one had the additional responsibilities of the specialist officer or leader, a flight commander or the commanding officer himself.

419 Squadron was flying the two-engined Wellington in 1942 under the leadership of its first CO, W/C John Fulton (brother of Davie, former MP). Fulton was shot down on 29 July and replaced by a Canadian serving in the RAF, W/C A.P. Walsh, DFC, AFC. Just seven weeks later, Walsh, too, was shot down and killed. Into this unhappy situation came RAF W/C Merv Fleming of Ottawa, who had been serving with the RAF since 1937 and who had won a DFC with 58 Squadron, RAF, in 1940.

The duties of a CO varied, but some tasks were traditional, and these were to make available each day the maximum possible number of aircraft and crews from the establishment of 20 aircraft, to bomb the allotted target accurately and to take such measures as necessary to achieve success over the target.

At the beginning of the working day and before it was known whether or not the unit would be required for operations, the CO called an informal meeting of his two flight commanders, the engineering officer, the armament officer and the squadron adjutant to determine squadron status. This meant aircraft serviceable for operations; number of aircraft that could be brought to operational serviceability by 1600 hours; availability of newly introduced or special-use equipment such as bombsights or navigational equipment; and training status of crews of aircraft. Availability of bombs of various types, mines, ammunition, pyrotechnics, photo flashes and cameras all had to be determined.

The CO and some of the other aircrew officers may well have been flying the night before, so stress upon such people was understandably extreme. Usually by mid-day, higher headquarters decided which squadrons were to go on a mission that night, to where, by what route, and what bomb load was to be carried. In 1942 the Commonwealth Air Forces were doing both day and night raids. A CO such as Merv then issued orders for the preparation of the battle order (crews and aircraft), fuel to be loaded, bombs or mines to be loaded, and for navigators to begin working out the routes to and from the target.

Merv Fleming's account continues:

Ops briefing was usually held around the dinner hour and was attended by the station commander, the two squadron commanders and the aircrews of both squadrons participating, as well as the meteorological officer and the intelligence officer. Unless there was a special message from the C-in-C or other special circumstances, the station commander took no active part in the briefing, but monitored the participation of the officers of his staff who proceeded to brief both squadrons on the weather, the defences and things to watch for. Each squadron commander then briefed his own people.

Depending upon the target, the weather, the bomb load and other considerations, the quiet hours between briefing and take-off could be "exhilarating or downright depressing". Letters to loved ones were written, superstitious routines were performed (Merv used to fully wind his alarm clock before leaving his room for the aircraft), and, finally, all operational aircrew enjoyed that ritual so often mentioned in other accounts -- the pre-op meal of bacon and eggs, otherwise scarce in England in those days.

The ride to the hangars was the first part of the long journey to the continent and back. Mae Wests, helmets and parachutes were taken from lockers and thence to dispersal points, where the aircraft were parked to reduce the effects of enemy attack on the aerodrome.

The aircraft were taxied nose to tail on either side of the entrance to the runway and then shut down till start-up time. If the CO was on the battle order, he became an aircraft skipper pure and simple. If time permitted, he usually visited the other crews (especially the new boys) to give them some encouragement, or crack a joke or two to relieve the tension, higher now than at any other time during the whole operation.

Merv continues:

On approach to the enemy coast all eyes were seeking a landfall pinpoint to correct one's heading and to warn of the first sign of flak. From this point to the target all microphones excepting those of the skipper and the tail gunner were kept in the "off" position to enable the pilot and gunner to take swift action in the event of an attack by fighters. Other crew members could, of course, open their mikes to transmit important information to any other crew member. While a great many crews believed in "jinking" their way to the target and back, quite a few others believed that unless the bursts were in front or you could hear the clatter of fragments on the aircraft skin or smell cordite, it was safer to do nothing that would interfere with accurate navigation or increase the time spent over enemy territory. Good navigation achieved both these desirable effects and afforded a good measure of protection from night fighters, who preferred to knock off stragglers. While one felt fairly calm on the run-in to the target, it had its psychological effects, and one almost universal manifestation of this was a desire to urinate. There are many stories about the difficulties of satisfying this urge, resulting in it being referred to as the "pre-target pee".

On the run-in to the target the bombaimer took effective control of the aircraft by instructing the pilot to "left-left", "or right 5 degrees", then, "Steady. Bomb door open. Bombs gone." And, finally, "Close bomb doors." If the bombs were released in a stick or in a pattern selected on a special dropping mechanism called a "Mickey Mouse", there was little effect on the trim of the aircraft on release. However, a release in salvo would certainly cause a bit of bucking since you were releasing up to 14,000 pounds at once.

Once the bombs had been released, the navigator set the course for the return trip. There was still no relaxation of attention, as all crew members kept a sharp eye for German fighters. Merv continues:

If and when a fighter attacked, one adopted an evasive tactic designed to destroy the attacker's aim while providing a good target for one's own gunners, and even if the chances of hitting him were poor, it could certainly discourage him. If the fighter approached from the port quarter, the tail gunner would say "dive port" and follow through the pattern by "up port, up starboard, down starboard" and repeating the process as often as required. These were violent manoeuvres for such large aircraft and resulted sometimes in dust and debris flying about and engines momentarily cutting out.

If all went well the aircrew would soon see the English Channel and then head for home. After landing everyone was debriefed by the intelligence officer, then, if they wanted it, given an issue of rum, then another meal of bacon and eggs. "And so to bed -- until we do it all over again tomorrow."

In an article in **Roundel**, S/L A.P. Heathcote wrote:

On 8 October [1943] after having guided the Moosemen for thirteen months, Merv Fleming was posted. It was fitting that this officer received the coveted DSO to add to his DFC. The citation [mentioned] an "ideal leader whose skill, courage, and a devotion to duty on a large number of difficult operations had contributed materially to the

115

operational efficiency of the squadron.

Merv Fleming returned home to Ottawa and joined the Department of Transport. He is now retired and spends his time in both Florida and Gatineau, Quebec. He attended the 1988 reunion of 419 Squadron in Cold Lake, Alberta: once again he was with the Moosemen.

W/C Merv Fleming at the time he was awarded the DSO

Air mechanic to lawyer

Claude Dingwall was just 19 when he enlisted in the RCAF in early 1941. His earliest recollection of Manning Depot in Toronto was that he was "somewhat in awe of the corporals who seemed to have God-like authority. The officers, by comparison were pussycats." Claude could not pass the aircrew medical, so he became an airframe technician. He saw his first aircraft some time later and was "in seventh heaven when taken up for a brief flight in a Harvard". Groundcrew training was at St Thomas, Ontario, where Claude learned to work on First War fabric-covered planes; "The hottest aircraft at the school was a Fairey Battle fighter."

On graduation from St Thomas, "96 out of a class of 98 volunteered to go overseas". An uneventful but rough crossing in November 1941 saw Claude posted to 403 Fighter Squadron, which was to be Claude's home for the next three years. The Mark V Spitfire was the aircraft in use with 403 Squadron, and half the pilots were RAF. The language of the RAF resulted in a new vocabulary for the Canadians in the groundcrew: "The aircraft was a kite, the gasoline tender a petrol bowser, and we aircraftmen were known as erks." The life of the groundcrew was one of working out in the open, and as 403 was a day fighter squadron it meant "work from pre-dawn to dark. In the summer months that was a 20-hour day."

In August the squadron moved to Manston, near Ramsgate, where it was to support the Dieppe Raid. On 19 August, Claude recalls,

> They worked like beavers throughout that long day, refuelling, re-arming and repairing. We maintained maximum serviceability. Our pilots claimed seven enemy aircraft destroyed, and from our perspective it was a most successful day.

In April 1944 Claude was moved to the south of England. He was still there on the 6th of June -- D-Day. 403 Squadron moved to France on D+6. Claude was flown over in a DC-3:

> It was a memorable sight below us. The entire Channel was chock full with ships. The battleships were lobbing shells far

inland. Our airstrip had been cut out of a farmer's field a day or so earlier. We arrived and were fully operational at once.

Claude and his fellow mechanics worked as normal, but with added interference for they were within range of German artillery and "every now and then a German plane would swoop over and strafe us. The steel helmet became very much in vogue."

By early autumn, 403 Squadron was in Holland near Grave. The Messerschmitt 262 German jet fighter was seen, and very soon the Spitfire pilots realized "it had a turn of speed that our fellows could not match". Adding to the problems of 403, "the rains came, and soon both men and machine were mired down."

Claude caught pneumonia and was hospitalized, but at year's end he rejoined his squadron. On New Year's Day "our airfield and several others were attacked by a horde of German fighters and fighter bombers. While personnel casualties were light, a large number of our aircraft were destroyed."

Unbeknownst to Claude, he was to get a big surprise on 28 January 1945. "I was told I was on a draft back to Canada the very next day." Things happened fast then. Claude arrived back in Montreal and was transferred to the Air Reserve on 1 April 1945. The war in Europe ended five weeks later.

Claude Dingwall went to Dalhousie University under veteran's credits, graduated in law and rejoined the RCAF in 1952. He retired from the Forces in 1975, served as a call-out until 1980 and then as a civilian lawyer in NDHQ until 1985. Today, he is retired and lives in Ottawa.

The Spitfire; the aircraft Claude maintained

Ferry Command duty

Bruce Beatty joined the RCAF in 1941 as a mechanic, but after a year he was taking aircrew training as an observer and bombaimer. In 1943 Bruce was at Lachine, Quebec, en route overseas. One night the entire draft "was called out in the middle of the night. We packed our kitbags aboard a truck and then handed in our bedding." When they were on the parade square getting ready to depart, 12 names were called out. Bruce's was one of them, and with the others he was detailed to return to barracks. "We sat and talked into the small hours and suddenly realized that each one of the 12 had started out as mechanics [fitters] or airframe mechanics [riggers]. After breakfast we were all sent to Dorval and told we were to be trained as flight engineers for multi-engine aircraft, and were to fly with Ferry Command." Bruce served with Ferry Command until the summer of 1944. He "flew to places in the U.S.A., flew a plane back to Gander, Newfoundland, and then other Ferry Command crews took the plane overseas."

In mid-1944 Bruce was sent to Pat Bay just north of Victoria, British Columbia, where he was to fly in Liberators and Hudsons on weather patrol and looking for Japanese fire balloons. "Our operations map was covered in coloured pins, which showed where these balloons landed. Some got as far as Northern Ontario." He continued to fly in Canada until 1945.

When the war ended, Sgt Beatty remained in the RCAF

Sgt Bruce Beatty in cold weather flying suit, 1942

as a mechanic, and in 1950 remustered to the graphic artist trade. He was still doing his wonderful drawings of badges and crests until he retired as a Master Warrant Officer in 1970. He then went to Rideau Hall to design Canada's medals.

Bruce Beatty is still with the Chancellery of Honours in Ottawa. In June 1990 Bruce was awarded the Order of Canada.

Fifty Years After

Chapter Five

The Home Front
(Women at war, at home and overseas)

In 1939 Canada's ability to manufacture weapons, vehicles, ammunition, ships and airplanes was almost non-existent. When reading about Canada at war, too small a reference is made to the transformation that took place at home. Shortages of trained men plus high casualties in the three services led to a call for the women of Canada to join the services and the civilian labour force.

In July 1941, the Canadian Women's Army Corps was created; the RCAF followed with the Canadian Women's Auxiliary Air Force, and in 1942 the RCN created the Women's Royal Canadian Naval Service. By 1945 the total number of women in the three services was over 45,000. An additional 4500 women were in the three medical services.

These women in uniform released men for tasks in the Army, RCN and RCAF in combat and the maintenance of the operational units overseas.

The civilian workforce also saw dramatic changes in the numbers of women performing duties to support the war effort. Canada's war effort surprised both Britain and the United States, for in no time Canada was producing armaments at the fourth highest level among the Allies. Forty thousand people worked in the shipyards by 1942, and double that number by 1944. Over 3000 ships of all kinds were launched from almost 100 shipyards. No civilian cars and trucks were built after 1941, but 3800 wheeled vehicles and 250 armoured vehicles a week were produced, as well as 315 aircraft a month. An ammunition production of millions of shells and small arms munitions rolled out of Canadian factories. As of 1943 only 30 percent of all the production went to the Canadian services, the rest to Britain, Russia and the other Allies.

The acceptance of women in the wartime labour force took longer to happen in the services than it did in industry, but in time praise such as "How did the service (RCAF) ever get along without them?" was common.

This quote from **The Canadians At War 1939/45** sums up the effect of women on the home front and overseas: "They proved their worth in the armed forces. They improved the status, morale and working conditions of their sex more than any social legislation had ever done. The implications are profound for the whole future of the family."

The story that follows of Joyce Bourne the cipher clerk is but one example of the home front -- strange jobs in strange places.

Secrets in New York

William Stephenson, "the man called Intrepid", figures in this story. In 1940, he was sent by Churchill to the United States to "establish top-level relations between the British Secret Intelligence Service (SIS) and the U.S. Federal Bureau of Investigation (FBI)." Out of this co-operation the British Security Co-ordination (BSC) was created. As the United States was neutral in this early stage of the war, its citizens could not be employed in war-related areas; thus, Canadians were in demand for such positions.

Joyce Bourne (her brother's story is in Chapter 4) was working for the Bank of Canada in Toronto when a friend said, "They're interviewing Canadians for positions with the BSC in New York; are you interested?" Joyce was, and a few days later she was interviewed by a Mrs Rowland of the BSC. "If I accepted they would provide accommodation for the first month, until we could find our own. It would be at the Allerton House for Women, not far from Rockefeller Centre." Later there was an interview with a Mrs Bowie, who gave Joyce a passport and a train ticket, with a date and time to report to BSC in the International Building in Rockefeller Centre. She went from Ottawa with another girl and they lived at Allerton House for that first month and then found a small apartment on 52nd Street:

> In New York we went to our hotel and reported the next day to the 35th floor of the International Building. We were interviewed by a Professor Rowland and Miss Edith Stewart Richardson, a tall, angular Scots woman of about 54 years. She explained the strict security that was necessary and that we could never even tell our grandchildren what we had done in the war. She would be my boss in the code room while the girl I came with was sent to the teletype room. I stayed on the 35th floor in the code room. The decoding was very difficult for me to learn. It was a great lesson in geography, mostly dealing with North and South America, Central America and London. There was a separate book for each country. We would decode the telegrams, type them up and then they were sent upstairs

125

to the 36th floor where Sir William Stephenson had his office. The room where we worked was small and each room was separate with no communication to the other rooms. The wireless room was off limits. When we worked at night we had to sign in and sign out in the lobby. It was always the same man at the desk; he was English and we called him Mr Lancashire (we did not know his real name).

Joyce McDonald 1940

In addition to these duties, the staff had an active social life, going to plays, theatres, museums and the Central Park Zoo. On two occasions they went to a dance given by the British for visiting Naval personnel; on one of these occasions the Duke and Duchess of Windsor put in an appearance. For a short period Sir Stafford Cripps's niece worked with BSC; when she was married she asked all of the ladies from the code room to her wedding, which was held in the Berkeley Hotel off Fifth Avenue. It was a real Naval wedding with officers lined up outside the hotel forming an arch with their swords.

Joyce described one event that is deep in her memory:

One night when I was on the midnight to 8 a.m. shift (when we were not usually as busy decoding telegrams as during the day), I received a message that I will never forget. It was from the agent in Montedvideo saying, "I have just been informed that my son has been shot down over Germany. Please confirm." The telegram went upstairs and that same night I had to send the reply, "We regret to confirm that your son was killed over Germany."

Joyce remembers more of the happy times than the sad. For instance, she was deeply impressed by the visits of Lord Louis Mountbatten and Baron Rothschild to the office. "On occasion, I would see Sir William, and I have the very lovely letter of recommendation signed by him that I was given when I left. It is a prized possession."

BSC closed its door when its requirements had been met. Joyce McDonald (nee Bourne) spent many years in the United States until she moved to Fitzroy Harbour, Ontario, where she is now living.

Fifty Years After

Epilogue

The Veteran

The experience of war has taught us that there are qualities and talents in all men which life never gave a chance.

G/C Leonard Cheshire, VC, DSO, DFC

This book is about average sailors, soldiers, airmen and women. They came from all walks of life, and most were very young. There is but one general in this book, Tommy Burns, and his story had a special place in my life: his wisdom and worldwide reputation as a peacekeeper make the bridge between the First and Second World Wars and Peacekeeping.

The people in **Fifty Years After** are all veterans, that band of brothers and sisters who volunteered to serve in Canada's forces during the 1939 -- 1945 period. Too many of them passed away while the book was in the making. My greatest pleasure was meeting most of them, asking them questions and recording their answers.

This is my tribute to Canadian veterans, to their wartime sacrifice, post-war suffering and combined contributions to Canada, their "home and native land".

As of mid-1989, almost 600,000 Second War veterans were still living. Those drawing pensions from Veterans Affairs numbered some 107,000 veterans plus about 65,000 widows. The average age of these special people will reach 70 years in 1990. Between 1 September 1939 and 30 September 1947, 45,600 Canadians and Newfoundlanders died because of the war. These figures form the statistical framework from which the stories in this book were drawn. Canada's veterans are from a generation who fought for their country, who believed in self-sacrifice of time, life and limb for one's country. Some suffered from the day of a wounding or sickness till the end of their days. Many became leaders of the nation or leaders in the business world. Some could never adjust to the changes demanded by life after wartime. In **The Veterans' Years**, Barry Broadfoot wrote that Canada "was the real winner, and the vets, with their desire to get ahead and their determination, have earned themselves a place of honour in Canada's hall of heroes. And I salute them." To this I can only add my sincere thanks for the stories so freely given to me from these veterans who, when given the chance, took it and made good.

Acknowledgements

During the research for this book many texts, biographies and unit histories were consulted. In the individual stories, quotations are given credit, but not footnoted. The most useful books from my own library are listed below, chapter by chapter.

Chapter One: World War Two: How did it all begin?

Reader's Digest The Canadians at War 1939/45 is a good source book, as is Desmond Morton's **A Military History of Canada** (Hurtig, 1985). A new book, **Courage Remembered** by G. Kingsley Ward and Edwin Gibson (HMSO, 1989), provides a different perspective on war. **Canadian Military Anecdotes** by Vic Suthern (Oxford University Press, 1989) provides vignettes from all services. The master of oral military history, Barry Broadfoot, has two books, **Six War Years 1939 - 1945** (Paper Jacks, 1974) and **The Veterans' Years** (Douglas and McIntyre, 1985). **Canadian War Stories** (Royal Canadian Legion, 1986) provided oral history from a different point of view. Finally, Alex Douglas and Ben Greenhous produced **Out of the Shadows** in 1977 to provide a synopsis of the total war effort.

Chapter Two: The Royal Canadian Navy

The official account of Canadian naval operations is Joseph Schull's **Far Distant Ships** (Stoddart, 1987, reprinted from 1950 version). Hal Lawrence's two books **A Bloody War** (Macmillan, 1979) and **Tales of the North Atlantic** (McLelland and Stewart, 1985) are the work of a master storyteller. **North Atlantic Run** by Marc Milner is a most factual book about the North Atlantic (University of Toronto Press, 1985). **Escort Commander** by Terence Robertson (Nelson Doubleday, 1979, reprinted from 1956 version) is a Royal Navy story, but it is of real value. James Lamb has two books **The Corvette Navy and On the Triangle Run** (Macmillan, 1986) -- both do justice to oral history. Two lengthy volumes of the biography of Jeffrey Brock **With Many Voices** and **The Thunder and the Sunshine** (McClelland and Stewart, 1981 and 1983) provide insight into war at sea and problems on land; the story of the unification of the Canadian Armed Forces is in the second volume. **50 North** (Paper Jacks, 1980) by Alan Easton explains the perils in the North Atlantic and the problems of a poorly equipped Navy. Finally, **U-Boat the Secret Menace** (Ballantine Books, 1968) by David Mason describes the major enemy at sea. **Salty Dips**, in three volumes, is great reading.

Chapter Three: The Canadian Army

The three-volume work including **Six Years of War** by C.P. Stacey, **Canadians in Italy** by G.W.H. Nicholson and **The Victory Campaign** by C.P. Stacey (Queen's Printer, 1955, 1956 and 1960) is an essential source book for any work of this nature. **The Canadian Army at War**, in three volumes -- **The Canadians in Britain 1939-1944, From Pachino to Ortona, Canada's Battle in Normandy** (King's Printer, 1944 and 1946) -- provides an overview taken from official records.

In no particular order, the following books provided insight into a battle or an individual act, be it in action or the actions surrounding a formation (Brigade or Division).

Farley Mowat's two books **The Regiment** (McLelland and Stewart, 1955) and **No Birds Sang** (1979) are two of the best "bird's-eye view" infantry stories, as is **The Long Road Home** by Fred Cederberg (Stoddart, 1985, reprinted from 1984 version). The Kiska invasions is well covered by Tony Foster in **Meeting of Generals** (Methuen, 1986). Hong Kong is also covered very well by Carl Vincent in **No Reason Why** (Canada's Wings, 1981). Reg Roy, one of Canada's best-known military historians, produced **1944: The Canadians in Normandy** (Macmillan, 1984) and **Ready for the Fray** (Evergreen Press, 1958). General Burns's book **General Mud** (Clarke, Irwin, 1970) was of great value on more than one occasion. The early history of The Canadian Armoured Fighting Vehicles School is covered in **Worthy** by Larry Worthington (T.H. Best, 1961). Padre stories are not numerous, but **The Padre** by Barry Rowland (Amethyst, 1982) gives insight into padres at war. **Six Armies in Normandy** by John Keegan (Penguin,

1982) and **Normandy to the Baltic** by Field Marshal Bernard Montgomery (British Army of the Rhine, 1946) give special understanding of the most famous of Second War land, sea and air battles.

Chapter Four: The Royal Canadian Air Force

I soon found that aircrew who had kept their wartime log books had a source of information of great value. **Bomber Harris** by Dudley Saward (Sphere Books, 1984) and **A Thousand Shall Fall** by Murray Peden (Canada's Wings, 1979) give a good insight into life in Bomber Command. **Lucky Thirteen** by Hugh Godefroy (Canada's Wings, 1983) did the same for fighter pilots. **Aerodromes of Democracy**: Canada and the British Commonwealth Air Training Plan -- 1939 - 1945 by Fred Hatch (Directorate of History, 1983) gives the details of a most successful RCAF operation here in Canada.

There were hundreds of pocket books and library books read during the research for this book, but the **Freedom's Battle** series by Arrow Books gives the reader a graphic account of warfare: **The War at Sea** by John Winton, **The War on Land** by Ronald Lewin; and **War in the Air** by Gavin Lyall (1970, 1971 and 1972).

My final acknowledgements go to Rachel Irwin and Wadad Bashour of Reader's Digest, Montreal, for their co-operation in allowing me to use **The Tools of War** drawings throughout this book. To Heather Ebbs, President of the Freelance Editors' Association of Canada and owner of Editor's Ink, Ottawa, for being my editor. To Tim Gordon and the staff of General Store Publishing House Inc. of Burnstown, Ontario, for their total involvement in publishing this book. To Veterans Affairs Canada for the statistics used in the epilogue and to Captain Wally Fowler and staff of the *Petawawa Post*. To General Dextraze, General Manson and Vice Admiral Fulton a very special thank you for reading the book in manuscript form and for writing such meaningful messages at the start of the book. Most of all, to my wife, Elaine, who typed the stories over and over for this my fourth book.

Fifty Years After

Index

About the Author

John Gardam has spent most of his life in uniform. He was born in England in 1931 and emigrated to Canada in 1946. He joined the Reserve Army in 1947 and the Regular Force as a Lord Strathcona's Horse Trooper four years later. He was commissioned in the Royal Canadian Dragoons in 1952.

During the next 32 years he served in Egypt with The Fort Garry Horse and in many places in Canada including The Royal Military College as Director of Cadets. He was made an officer of the Order of Military Merit in 1980. He received a degree in History from the University of Manitoba in 1979.

On retiring from the military in 1984 Colonel Gardam spent five years with the Commonwealth War Graves Commission. He is currently Project Director of the DND Peacekeeping Monument in Ottawa.

John and his wife Elaine live in Nepean, Ontario. They have four sons and four grandchildren.